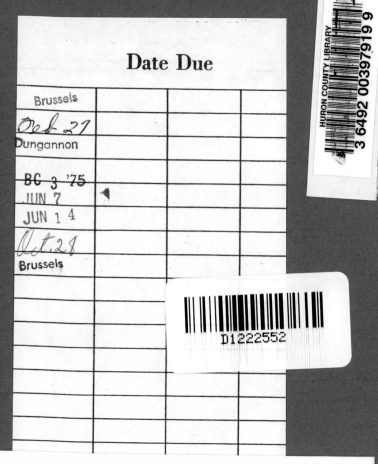

Date Due

Brussels			
Oct 21			
Dungannon			
BC 3 '75			
JUN 7			
JUN 1 4			
Oct. 28			
Brussels			

D1222552

The Death of Hockey

The
Death
of Hockey

Bruce Kidd and John Macfarlane

new press
TORONTO
1972

ISBN 88770-102-7

Jacket Design by Ralph Tibbles and Jon Eby

Manufactured in Canada by
The Alger Press Limited

*For the rightful owners of
hockey, the Canadian people.*

A typical amateur hockey player of about 1922.

We sit up there in the blues
bored and sleepy and suddenly three men
break down the ice in roaring feverish speed and
we stand up in our seats with such a rapid pouring
of delight exploding out of self to join them why
theirs and our orgasm is the rocket stipend
for skating through the smoky end boards out
of sight and climbing up the appalachian highlands
and racing breast to breast across laurentian barrens
over hudson's diamond bay and down the treeless
                              tundra where
auroras are tubercular and awesome and
stopping isn't feasible or possible or lawful
but we have to and we have to
                    laugh because we must and
stop to look at self and one another but
            our opponent's never geography
                or distance why
                    it's men
                        —just men?

from Hockey Players, by Al Purdy

Acknowledgements

This book was inspired by the example of two men: Father David Bauer, former coach of Canada's National Team, and Bill L'Heureux, former chairman of the National Advisory Council for Fitness and Amateur Sport. We are also greatly indebted to Jim Bacque, Peter C. Newman, Michael de Pencier, Maxine Crook, Bernadette Sulgit and many others for their advice, assistance and encouragement. To all of them we say thank you.

For permission to reproduce excerpts, we thank the following authors and publishers: *Hockey in Canada: The Way It Is!* by Brian Conacher, Gateway Press Limited, Toronto 1970; *A Dream of Lilies* by Joan Finnigan, The Fiddlehead, Fredericton 1965; *Hello, Canada, and Hockey Fans in the United States* by Foster Hewitt, Thomas Allen Limited, Toronto 1950; *Strength Down Centre* by Hugh Hood, Prentice-Hall of Canada, Ltd., Scarborough 1970; *50 Years of Hockey* by Brian McFarlane, Pagurian Press Limited, Toronto 1967; *The Caribou Horses* by Al Purdy, McClelland and Stewart Limited, Toronto 1965; and *Road to Olympus* by Anatoli Tarasov, Griffin House, Toronto 1969.

Contents

The Canadian Specific

It is February, and in Toronto the days are short and grey, the snow dirty and cheerless. Maybe it will be better in Winnipeg. You have business there, and the air traffic controllers are on strike so you are taking the train. It is nine o'clock at night, and the train has stopped in a small town in northwestern Ontario. The wood frame station is the only building larger than a house. Not many people live here, probably fewer this year than last, and from the train window you can see houses boarded up. It is below zero outside, a blizzard has dumped four feet of clean snow, and the town probably has never looked better than it does now through the darkness and the snow and the steam that drifts up from the train past your window. It is quiet. There are only two signs of life, only one if you do not count the presence of the train which will be somewhere else in 15 minutes. A few hundred yards from the tracks, on the town side of the tracks, cleared of snow and lit up like a small-town used car lot, there is a hockey rink — old boards carefully nailed together to form a wooden rectangle around a sheet of natural ice. A dozen men and boys, oblivious to the cold and the town and the train, are playing hockey.

Hockey is the Canadian metaphor, the rink a symbol of this country's vast stretches of water and wilderness, its extremes of climate, the player a symbol of our struggle to civilize such a land. Some people call it our national religion. Well, what better? Like the ball games of the Mayan Indians of Mexico, worshipped because the arc of the kicked ball was thought to imitate the flight of the sun and moon across the heavens, hockey captures the essence of the Canadian experience in the New World. In a land so inescapably and inhospitably cold, hockey is the dance of life, an affirmation that despite the deathly chill of winter we are alive.

To speak of a national religion, of course, is to grope for a national identity. We in English Canada have always been uncertain of our identity because we have always been a colony, first of the British Empire and now of the American, sharing in each case a common language and a similar history. In the Nineteenth Century, we saw ourselves as a British outpost in North America. Today we are being assimilated into the homogenizing frontier traditions of the United States. (By comparison, Québec, with a distinct language, religion and economic history, has never doubted its individuality.) Our cultural and historical experience is unique, but our ties to one empire or another have blinded us to the fact. Except for hockey, which the late Ralph Allen used to describe as the one true Canadian invention. Unsure as we are about who we are, we know at least this about ourselves: we are hockey players, and we are hockey fans, and once we could say we were the best.

Hockey is something most of us share almost from birth. From the frost of October to the thaws of April, in the outports of Newfoundland, the rural villages of Québec and the manufacturing cities of Ontario, in the prairie towns of Saskatchewan and the trailer camps of northern British Columbia, boys learn to skate propped up by hockey sticks. Canadian fathers brag that their sons learn to skate before they walk, a revealing lie, and it is the deprived Canadian boy who does not once get a hockey stick for Christmas. The game is a national puberty rite, performed by wobbly-legged kids for congregations of rink-side parents. What is Canada? A country of 250,000 kids getting up at seven o'clock on Saturday morning for a game in a dingy concrete block arena, dreaming of the day when their red, white and blue Canadiens hockey socks will be real instead of the kind anyone can buy out of Eaton's catalogue.

A boy learns more than stickhandling at the community arena. Hockey, as a unique expression of our culture, is also a vessel for its values, passing them father-to-son from one generation to the next. In the corners and along the boards, in the dressing rooms and on the bench, in the clash of body against body, wood and ice, a boy learns our attitudes towards team play, fair play and dirty play, towards winning and losing, tolerance and prejudice, success and failure. "Break the rules and you'll get a penalty — if you're caught." It is through hockey that a Canadian boy first perceives his geographic horizons. He knows there is another part of town because he has played hockey there, and that Canada stretches across the Prairies and the Rocky Mountains to the Pacific because that is where Vancouver is, and Vancouver has Dale Tallon. And it is through hockey, through the encouragement of his family and friends and the entreaties of his coaches, that he learns that apart from his own desires and ambitions he must live with the expectations of others. Hockey also teaches him the difference between boys and girls. In 1956 nine-year-old Abigail Hoffman, who went on to become one of Canada's greatest Olympic athletes, played defence for the St. Catharines Teepees in the Little Toronto Hockey League. When it was discovered she was a girl she was immediately dropped from the team. Playing hockey is for boys. Girls are permitted only to watch. In school a boy learns what we profess to believe. In hockey he learns what we really believe.

All this is to show that for Canadians, hockey is more than just entertainment. It has a significance here it has nowhere else in the world, like bullfighting in Spain or cooking in France. But it is not for its significance that we love the game. We love it because it is one of the most beautiful games in the world. The exhilaration of rink-long rushes in the chilling air. The satisfaction of a well-delivered body check. The special elation of scoring a goal, that thrilling culmination of physical and mental reflex, wit, discipline — and sometimes luck. Hockey is all of these things, but it is first the sheer pleasure of skating. Eric Nesterenko, who played 21 years in the National Hockey League, rhapsodized: "Some nights you just go. You can't stop. The rhythm gets to you, or the speed. You're moving, man, moving, and that's all." You do not have to play hockey professionally to experience that feeling. Novelist Hugh Hood, who plays once a week in a Montreal industrial league, describes it like this: "Once or twice a season I'll hit a point where my skating comes together. There is no physical feeling I know of that is quite like that, and only one that's better. When my skating finally comes right, it isn't a short intense pleasure, it's a long slow one spread over my whole body, a sense of great health and well-being. My legs seem to be swinging loose from the hip in a long stride that eats up rink space, and my breathing is close to what it would be if I had the guts to give up smoking. Making love is even better, but next to it comes the feeling of skating freely, as if you could go on for hours and never feel fatigue."

Skating makes hockey one of the most sensual of sports, which is why so many of us play it. But it is also among the most creative. Not as programmed as baseball or football, where offences and defences are carefully worked out in advance, so that the game becomes largely a question of execution. Faster than those other wonderfully spontaneous games, soccer, rugger and basketball (a man can skate almost twice as fast as he can run, and a puck can be shot at more than 150 feet per second). In hockey, plays are conceived and executed instantly, almost instinctively. "When I carry the puck across the blueline," says Dave Keon, "I've got less than a second to choose from any of a hundred plays I could make to try and get by the opposing defencemen." Rushing, stickhandling, backchecking, diving, rushing, passing, backchecking, rushing — the basic plays are obvious and simple and they are repeated endlessly, but never in the same way or in the same sequence. So when the puck is dropped for a faceoff, whether it is the Canadiens in the Montreal Forum or the neighbourhood kids on the street, something different happens every time.

That is the magic of hockey, its unlimited dramatic possibilities. And that is what makes it almost as exciting a game to watch as it is to play. The spectator cannot experience the game the way the players do. And maybe it is true, as some pro hockey players insist, that anyone who has not played the game professionally sees only half of what takes place on the ice. But there are compensations. The spectator sees the game as a whole, like someone watching a game of two-handed poker, knowing each player's cards. The spectator experiences more fully the subtleties of physical expression different players bring to the game — the grace of Frank Mahovlich, turning in his own end, starting up the ice with long, flowing strides; the self-assurance of Bobby

Orr, whose command of the game's basic skills is so sure that he can do anything it occurs to him to do at the instant it occurs to him to do it; the speed and flair of Yvan Cournoyer, racing into the clear between two helpless defencemen; the bravado of a Jacques Plante, who can make even the easiest saves seem dramatic. Only the spectator can appreciate the abstract beauty of the game — the ebb and flow of bodies drawn this way and that by the puck, like iron filings arranging and rearranging themselves around an elusive black magnet.

More Canadians watch hockey — in the streets, at rinks and on television — than engage in any other single public activity. More Canadians watch hockey now than go to church. *Hockey Night in Canada* really *is* hockey night in Canada. We schedule our lives around it. During elections, Canadian political parties tell their canvassers not to knock on doors during hockey games, because to interrupt a hockey fan at his pleasure is almost certainly to lose his vote. At playoff time, Canadian churches hold their services early so their congregations can get home in time for the Sunday afternoon game. And at Canadian universities, where final examinations and playoffs have a tendency to coincide, there is an inevitable exodus from libraries and study halls just before game time, even scholarly discipline having its limits. How many Canadians watch the Saturday night hockey telecast? The CBC says 6 million, 10 million during the playoffs. A Montreal taxi driver will tell you that on Saturday nights he can practically set his watch by the slack period that begins with the opening faceoff at eight o'clock and ends when the game is over around 10:30. It is said of virtually every Canadian city that during a hockey telecast its consumption of water increases perceptibly between periods.

It was the same in the beginning. Old-timers tell stories about how they used to bundle themselves up to stand in sub-zero winds watching hockey on outdoor rinks. It was not until 1911, when Frank and Lester Patrick introduced artificial ice to Vancouver and Victoria, where natural ice is a sometimes thing, that hockey fans were afforded shelter from the elements. Even in the covered arenas, symbols of community prosperity, doors and windows were left wide open to keep the ice good and frozen. Likewise, of course, the fans. And in those days, years before radio and television, getting the results of an out-of-town series was not the easy thing it is today. When the Toronto Wellingtons went to Winnipeg for the 1902 Stanley Cup series against the Winnipeg Victorias, thousands of fans stood in the cold outside the King Street offices of the Toronto *Globe* where a running account of each game was relayed by CPR telegraph. And when each game was over, *The Globe* sent a courier to the Toronto street railway powerhouse, where the name of the winner was relayed to the waiting city by a prearranged signal — two whistles signifying a Toronto victory, three whistles a Toronto defeat.

To this day, hockey remains a universally understood language in a country where the English do not speak French and the French do not speak much English, in which Britain is still referred to as "the old country" and Maritimers call people in Ontario "Upper Canadians". Hockey spans the distances, cultural and topographical, that separate the 22 million people who inhabit these 3,851,809 square miles of land and fresh water. If it was the CPR and the wheat economy that encouraged culture to flow east and west instead of north and south during the first 70 years of Canada's existence, *Hockey Night in Canada* has played much the same role ever since. Foster Hewitt began broadcasting the Toronto Maple Leafs Saturday night hockey games to CBC listeners across the country in 1931. During one such broadcast in 1937, his audience was estimated at more than 6 million — which, if true, means that more than half the people in the country, men, women and children, were for a few hours that night united around their radios. The popularity of those Saturday night broadcasts was astonishing. There was one year when Hewitt received 90,000 fan letters. "They streamed in from all across the country," he has recalled. "From a lighthouse on the Bay of Fundy, a trawler on the North Atlantic fishing banks, a dormitory in a Maritime ladies college, a Hudson's Bay trading post far north of Churchill, a theatre in a French Canadian community in North Alberta, a construction camp many miles from rail in Northern Ontario, a barber shop in a small Saskatchewan village, an isolated British Columbia home where mail arrived only once a month." It did not matter that Hewitt described the game in a verbal shorthand because his listeners knew hockey so well they could fill in the detail for themselves. It was the Saturday night hockey audience that launched Canadian television, providing CBC-TV, not otherwise notably successful in developing popular Canadian programming, with a ready-made national audience. Hockey came to television in 1954, when a TV set was a community resource, like a newspaper during the Depression and a backyard swimming pool today. If you were a boy in those days, you really worked at your friendship with the kid whose parents were the first on the block with TV. To offend him was to risk not being invited into his living room on Saturday night to watch the hockey game. The Montreal Canadiens were emerging as the golden team of hockey back then, with Rocket Richard, Elmer Lach, Boom Boom

Geoffrion, Bert Olmstead, Doug Harvey and young stars like Jean Beliveau and Jacques Plante. And in Montreal, even on the coldest and snowiest of winter nights, people would stand outside appliance store windows watching the Rocket, Boom Boom and Le Gros Bill on TV. Sometimes a thoughtful store owner would provide benches of barrels and old boards.

It was only natural that hockey players should have become our national folk heroes. Hockey, after all, was the only popular culture we did not import. Lacking the initiative and self-confidence to create alternatives to Broadway, Hollywood and Tin Pan Alley, Canadians assumed until very recently that all the great actors, film stars and popular singers were Americans (or Canadians who became Americans). We ignored our writers. Morley Callaghan is better known to Canadians as a panelist on *Fighting Words,* the radio quiz show of the 1950s, than as one of the best North American novelists of his generation. And of the handful of celebrities Canadian television has produced, the majority have been, not artists, but journalists. So it is not surprising that compared to hockey players like Syl Apps, Maurice Richard and Gordie Howe, our artists and intellectuals have lived in relative obscurity. It is doubtful that any Canadian, including the Prime Minister, would be recognized by more people on the main street of a Canadian town or city than Gordie Howe. Although he was born and raised in Floral, Saskatchewan, for more than 20 years he has lived in Detroit, where he was a star with the Detroit Red Wings. But in Moncton and Lennoxville, Sault Ste. Marie and North Battleford, Red Deer and Powell River, Gordie Howe is still regarded as one of our own. Howe tells a story about a fishing trip he made a few years ago to a place north of Edmonton called Moose Lake. He was driving across a bridge and rolled down the car window to talk to a man fishing over the side. "How are they biting?" he asked. The man turned, and as if he and Howe were next-door neighbours, replied: "Pretty good, Gord."

Hockey players like Howe are for Canadians everything that actors like Paul Newman, television stars like Johnny Carson, and athletes like Joe Namath, Muhammad Ali, Johnny Bench and Arnold Palmer are for Americans. We revere them not only for their mastery of hockey, but also for the wealth and acclaim that go with it. We begrudge our Members of Parliament $28,000 a year, we balk at giving a $9,000-a-year teacher a $500 increase, but when Bobby Hull negotiates a $2.8 million contract we are delighted, because Hull, after all, is one of us, only better, and his success symbolizes the possibility, however remote, that wealth and acclaim might be ours too. Later on, perhaps, a Canadian boy with ambition sees himself as a doctor, lawyer, chairman of the board, maybe even prime minister, but while he is still a boy and can still make the team, he sees himself as a hockey star, because a hockey star is the one true Canadian celebrity.

And that is just as true for the son of a Montreal millionaire as it is for the son of a poor Saskatchewan farmer, because hockey bridges not only the cultural and topographical distances between us but the social and economic distances as well. In another country, a bank teller and a bank president might discuss, for want of anything else, the weather. Here they would talk about last night's hockey game. Hockey is the Canadian universal, neither sport of kings nor of peasants. It is everybody's sport, no matter what their class. Of course, class is a concept we do not talk about in Canada. It is hardly ever mentioned in government reports on poverty, housing, unemployment and family breakdown, because it is contrary to the popular mythology that any poor boy who works hard enough can make himself a bundle. Still, it exists, and we all know it, and it has played an important part in the evolution of hockey.

The upper classes, the people who run the country — bankers and businessmen, publishers and stockbrokers, doctors, lawyers and engineers — have been hockey's great patrons. It was in the regiments, universities and private clubs that the game first flourished. In the 1890s, for example, some of the best hockey in Toronto was played at the Granite Club, whose members, then as now, comprised a healthy representation of the city's wealthy families. The teams had names like the Viceregals and the Victorias and, in some cases, were made up of the employees of banks and insurance companies. (It is worth noting, if only to dispel the notion that hockey was a gentlemanly sport until it took hold in the mining towns, that some of those Granite Club games were not very sporting. "It is greatly to be regretted," observed a reporter for *The Globe* in an account of a game between the Parliamentary and Viceregal teams, "that in a game between amateur teams some players should so forget themselves before such a number of spectators, a good proportion of whom on the occasion referred to being ladies, as to indulge in fisticuffs, and the action of some spectators in rushing on the ice is also to be deplored.") Later on the game became a national pastime, loved as much by wage earners as by men of means, but even then it was the merchants and businessmen who supported it, by sponsoring teams outright, or by helping to write off a post-season debt. And when it became apparent that there was money to be made in hockey, it was the merchants and businessmen who turned the game professional, putting together teams of outstanding amateur players who were only too happy to leave little towns across the country to become paid hockey players. No one knew back then that professional hockey would eventually take a stranglehold on the game. But that is how it has turned out, and in that sense hockey is not very different now from what it was when it was played in the Granite Club. It is still the plaything of the rich.

For working-class Canadians, hockey has been something quite different. For them, it has been an escape, a physical antidote to the drudgery of modern industrial routine, a respite from the uncertainties of unemployment and poverty. Hockey has been an escalator out of a boring world of living wages into a dream world of big money and fast cars, tailored suits and sirloin steaks, interviews and autographs and girls. It is only natural that most of the players who make it to professional hockey should come from working-class homes. They work at it harder, because they have more to gain. And, like their parents, they have fewer diversions. If you have money, there are a lot of things you can do on Saturday night. You can go out to dinner, take in a show — if you have money you can do anything you want. If you do not, you can watch the hockey game. It is not just Gallic temperament that makes French Canadians the most tenacious of fans; it is the fact that for two centuries they have been the most economically deprived people in Canada. In the summer, wealthy Quebeckers go to their summer homes in the Laurentians; for the workers there is baseball or perhaps the horses. In the winter, Quebeckers with money ski or take the sun in Miami; for the workers there is hockey. *Of course* they take it seriously. In March, 1955, 10,000 Montreal fans, angered by NHL President Clarence Campbell's suspension of Rocket Richard, went berserk, sweeping down Ste. Catherine Street, wrecking cars, burning newsstands, overturning telephone booths, looting store windows.

They care about hockey; perhaps they care too much, but it is not so different for working-class people elsewhere in Canada. In 1963, the late Stafford Smythe, who was then president of the Toronto Maple Leafs, let it slip that television coverage of Toronto's Wednesday night games might be discontinued the following year in favour of a closed circuit network of theatres with large-screen TV projectors. "Who knows," he said, "maybe it will mean the end of watching the Saturday night spectacular from the living-room armchair." The next day a reporter asked Spencer Caldwell, then president of CTV, the network that carries the Wednesday night games, what he thought of Smythe's speculation. Caldwell is a realistic man. He said he doubted that Smythe or anyone else connected with big league hockey would cut off television coverage because the game "is more important in tens of thousands of rural homes across the continent — especially in the cold of the Prairies — than it is for us big-city types who might have the money to buy a ticket to the Gardens or a TV-equipped movie house." If TV hockey coverage were terminated, said Caldwell, it would set off a chain reaction and "heaven alone knows where it might end".

Yes, hockey is the Canadian metaphor, and those who dismiss it as only a game miss its meaning. Social historian Bruce Hutchison, who once travelled with Lester Patrick's Victoria Cougars as a public relations man, puts it this way: "Hockey is very important to Canada in a sense above and beyond politics. It has a psychological effect on the nation more important than many of the lofty political ideals we pretend to believe in." But if hockey is a metaphor for what is right with Canada, it is also a metaphor for what is wrong. Hockey has come to symbolize our capitulation to the economic realities as surely as it does our triumph over the physical ones. We live in a country we no longer own. We merely lease it from the Americans. We have sold them our oil and gas, our minerals, our forests and most of our industry. We have allowed them to assume control of parts of our universities and some of our publishing houses. We buy American magazines, we watch American films and television programmes, we eat in American-franchised restaurant chains, we sleep in American hotels, and we probably will be buried by American undertakers. And what of hockey? Saturday night is still hockey night in Canada. There is still a Hewitt in the broadcast booth at Maple Leaf Gardens. There is still a waiting list of thousands for season's tickets at the Montreal Forum. Kids still collect hockey cards. And in towns like Floral, Parry Sound and Trois Rivières they still dream of scoring goals under television lights in Montreal, Toronto and Vancouver. But if they make it, they will play most of their hockey in Boston, New York, Philadelphia, Pittsburgh, Detroit, Chicago, Minneapolis, St. Louis, Los Angeles, Oakland, Long Island and Atlanta. We may still call it our national game, but like nearly everything else in this country we have sold it to the Americans.

Of the 51 professional hockey teams now operating in North America, 45 are owned by Americans; 43 play in American cities. In addition to the National Hockey League cities, and those of the new World Hockey Association, there are professional hockey teams, and pretty good teams at that, in such American cities as Providence (population: 179,-116), Syracuse (population: 197,208), Springfield (population: 163,905), Rochester (population: 296,233), Hershey (population: 6,851), Tulsa (population: 330,350), Omaha (population: 346,929), Phoenix (population: 581,562), Portland (population: 380,620), Oklahoma City (population: 368,856), and Amarillo (population: 127,010). In

16

any of those cities and a dozen more you can see better hockey (played by Canadians) than you can in such Canadian cities as St. John's (population: 86,290), London (population: 221,430), Windsor (population: 199,784), Hamilton (population: 307,473), Thunder Bay (population: 107,805), Regina (population: 137,759), Saskatoon (population: 125,079), Calgary (population: 400,154), Victoria (population: 60,897). It may be our national religion, but the services are held in the United States.

Oh, we may comfort ourselves with the knowledge that 95 per cent of the players in professional hockey are Canadians. Those are still our boys out there, making the big plays and skating pretty, turning them on in Los Angeles, New York and in between, showing all those fat men with cigars in their mouths and bourbon in their bellies a better game than their baseball and their football. But what does that say about us? What kind of people force their best young athletes, their national heroes, to pursue their careers in another country? No wonder we are apathetic, even defeatist, about the country's future. No wonder we lack the courage to defend ourselves against such economic assaults as Nixonomics. No wonder our best actors, artists and musicians are compelled to seek recognition in the United States. Every day we tell ourselves that what happens in Canada does not really count. Nowhere is that more apparent than in hockey.

Besides, how long will it be before the Americans no longer want our hockey players? In the last decade, the number of boys playing hockey in the United States has increased so dramatically that within a few years, perhaps less than 10, half or more of the rookies in professional hockey will be Americans. Unlike us, Americans protect their jobs. In college hockey they are doing it already. The National Collegiate Athletic Association is making it more and more difficult for Canadians to play for American universities. It has recently ruled, for instance, that anyone who has played Junior "A" hockey in Canada is ineligible.

And even if Canadians continue to dominate pro hockey's playing ranks, a hockey player is ultimately just an employee, paid to do as he is told, even if he earns $100,000 a year. So the *employees* are overwhelmingly Canadian, the *employers* are overwhelmingly American, and in hockey, as in any other business, it is the employer who calls the shots. The 16 governors of the NHL, 14 of whom are Americans, are the real masters of hockey today, and if to accommodate an American television network they decide that Stanley Cup playoff games should be played on Sunday afternoon instead of Saturday night (which they have), who is Bobby Orr or Frank Mahovlich or Phil Esposito or Rod Gilbert or Stan Mikita or Yvan Cournoyer, all good Canadians and true, to tell them they cannot? And if they decide, as sooner or later it is logical they should, that at least half of the million dollars a year the NHL contributes to the support of amateur hockey in Canada should be invested in American amateur hockey instead, well, we have got only two votes after all, and business is business.

Hockey began to die— as a Canadian game—in 1908 when Sir H. Montagu Allan offered a cup to the best senior amateur team in the country and the Stanley Cup was turned over to the professionals. In 1926, it became the exclusive property of the National Hockey League—private property belonging, not as Lord Stanley had intended, to the men who played the game, but to the men who owned it. Hockey had been condemned to the marketplace where anything that is profitable is possible — even selling out.

As with so many of our resources, the sellout of hockey was the inevitable consequence of our proximity to the

United States and our cheap faith in free enterprise. What kind of goods we consume, how long we work, what kind of television we watch, how much we spend on roads and schools, how much pollution we tolerate — all these decisions we leave to the marketplace. Hockey, as just one more commodity in the marketplace, was fair game. Once it became no more than a business, like selling soap, every major decision — the length of the schedule, the rules, the draft, expansion — could be reduced to one simple question: How will it affect the profits? And because the Americans could afford to pay more for hockey than we could, they got it.

Turning hockey from a game into a business has benefited neither the fans, the players nor the game itself. Only the owners, who to maximize their profits created a monopoly called the National Hockey League so they could charge as much as they wanted for as many seats as they wanted to sell. Until the advent of the World Hockey Association, the NHL deliberately and systematically eliminated any challenge to its domination of the game. Who knows how many professional hockey teams might be playing in Canada today had it not been for the determination of the Montreal Canadiens and the Toronto Maple Leafs to see that they did not? It has been great for the shareholders, but it has exiled millions of Canadian hockey fans to the television set. And it has turned the game's best players into entertainers. No athlete, no matter how talented, no matter how well-conditioned, can perform at anything close to his potential when he is playing 105 games in an eight-month season and, between games, logging 100,000 miles in air. And while salaries have tripled in recent years, players are nevertheless subject to the mindless authoritarianism of coaches like Punch Imlach. It is no wonder that Bobby Hull, who has become a millionaire playing hockey, can say "the game isn't fun anymore". As for the game itself, its decline is painfully obvious. Sportsmanship, skill and beauty have been sacrificed for profit. Professional hockey has abandoned the grace and style so natural in a skating-passing game because, as everyone knows, winning teams sell more tickets than losing teams, and if you cannot win the way you are supposed to, win any way you can. So it is clutch and grab and, failing everything else, fight. Thus the Wayne Cashmans and Rosaire Paiements, the bullies professional hockey celebrates — ironically — as "policemen". There are more young people playing hockey today than ever before, and with hockey schools and coaching clinics they are getting better coaching. But they are being taught not only how to skate and shoot but how to hold and fight. The example of professional hockey has poisoned the game.

And so the death of hockey. How it happened and what we can do about it — that is what this book is about.

Watering Down
the Whisky

On Saturday nights at precisely 7:30, the six-year-old boy would have a bath. Sometimes he'd lie very still and the water would become a sheet of ice, the white sides of the bathtub being the boards. Streaking down the left wing, stick-handling around one defenceman, faking the other to the ice, then cutting sharply towards the net and beating the goalie with a shoulder-high wrist shot to the stick side, was the player he himself would be some day if only he could stop from going over on his ankles .

In the bathtub there was no overtime. The game always ended at 10 minutes to eight. The boy would climb out of the tub, walk to his bedroom and turn on the brown plastic mantle radio on the table beside his bed. Then he would climb into bed. When the radio had warmed up, he would tune it to the CBC, and then, with perhaps two minutes to go, he would remove the red elastic band from the four-inch-thick bundle of hockey cards he had brought with him to bed.

The cards came wrapped in wax-paper with a flat pink square of grainy bubble-gum. The cards never seemed to lose the cheap, sweet aroma of the gum, and the gum always tasted faintly of cardboard. But 10 cents, a week's allowance, would buy two packs of cards at the corner variety store, where they were a big item (along with candy cigarettes). You never knew whom you were buying. In any 10-cent purchase there might be a journeyman like Rudy Migay or Ray Timgren, Fern Flaman or Gus Mortson, but there might just as easily be a star like Ted Kennedy or Elmer Lach, Max Bentley or Milt Schmidt. Somewhere there's a self-made millionaire whose appetite for profit was whetted as a boy trading one Turk Broda for two Sugar Jim Henrys and future considerations.

And then it was eight o'clock and Jack Dennett would be saying ". . . and Esso dealers from coast to coast bring you Hockey Night in Canada." The boy would put aside the cards of all but two teams, the Toronto Maple Leafs and whomever they were playing that night. And then Foster Hewitt: "Hello Canada and hockey fans in the United States . . ." The voice — tinny and nasal like an old gramophone record, somehow disembodied and floating around the steel rafters of Maple Leaf Gardens. The boy would be lining up the two sets of cards, the Maple Leafs on one side of the bed, the opposing team on the other, as the voice sang out, more like a priest beginning Mass than a sportscaster starting his windup, "Tonight, from Maple Leaf Gardens, the Toronto Maple Leafs versus . . ." And for the next two-and-a-half hours, as the voice described the game, the boy would recreate it on his bed. Saturday night was the best night of the week.

Years later, when he was lucky enough to get tickets for a Maple Leaf home game, he would prefer to sit in the end zones where the sightlines corresponded more or less to the perspective he had of the hockey card game that was played on his bed. But it was never the same. Was it his imagination, or had hockey lost the magic it had for him as a boy?

Somehow, sitting in Maple Leaf Gardens, he always felt cheated.

In 1905, the hottest team in hockey was the Ottawa Silver Seven. Led by a dapper centre named Frank McGee, the Silver Seven had won the Stanley Cup, then only 13 years old, three years in a row. Ottawa hockey fans would jam the old Gladstone Avenue Arena and shout "McGee! McGee! McGee!" as the blond centreman, his white pants pressed to a knife edge, his boots shined and his stick freshly taped, executed his favourite play: taking the puck near his own defence, plunging through the opposing team at blinding speed, and driving home a goal. In a Stanley Cup playoff game that year against the Dawson City Nuggets (they came by dog team to Skagway, by boat to Vancouver and by train to Ottawa, a distance of 4,000 miles in 30 days), McGee scored 14 such goals — eight of them in eight minutes and 20 seconds. The Ottawa Senators won five more Stanley Cups — in 1909, 1911, 1920-21, 1923 and 1927. Those were great years for Ottawa hockey fans. Then in 1934, owner Frank Ahearn sold the Ottawa franchise to St. Louis. It happened that quickly: one year Ottawa fans were watching stars like McGee, Hooley Smith, Frank Finnigan and King Clancy play the best hockey in the world, the next year nothing. For years after, the only hockey to speak of in Ottawa was junior hockey.

Ottawa's story is the story of hockey in dozens of Canadian cities and towns. Not so many years ago, good senior hockey was played in places like Penticton, Lethbridge, Kenora, Sault Ste. Marie, Windsor, Belleville, Trois Rivières, Saint John and Sydney. Some of the best hockey this country has ever seen was played by teams like the Victoria Cougars, the Vernon Canadians, the Kelowna Packers, the Calgary

Stampeders, the Edmonton Flyers, the Saskatoon Quakers, the Regina Rangers, the Selkirk Fishermen, the Winnipeg Monarchs, the Red Lake Thunderers, the Kirkland Lake Blue Devils, the Sudbury Tigers, the Owen Sound Mercuries, the Chatham Maroons, the London Battery, the Kitchener Greenshirts, the Hamilton Tigers, the Toronto National Sea Fleas, the Montreal Victorias, the Quebec Aces, the Moncton Hawks, the Kentville Wildcats, the Halifax Wolverines, and the Charlottetown Abegweits. Today, in these and many other Canadian communities, the fans have only the dregs of semi-professional hockey or junior hockey or no hockey at all. They still produce good hockey players, but as soon as they are of age, they are shipped off to be groomed for the National Hockey League or — now — the World Hockey Association. Big league professional hockey is played in only eight Canadian cities: in Vancouver, Toronto and Montreal, which have NHL franchises; in Edmonton, Winnipeg, Ottawa and Quebec City, which have WHA franchises; and in Halifax, which has a franchise in the American Hockey League. Eight teams in eight cities, where once there were many times that number in towns and cities across the country. Which raises a terrible truth: in the country which calls hockey its national sport, there are millions of fans who have never seen a well-played game except on television. How could we have allowed that to happen?

Thunder Bay, the combined municipalities of Fort William and Port Arthur, is bigger and busier than a town and yet not quite a city, like so much of Canada beyond the limits of Vancouver, Toronto and Montreal. Hugging the shores of Lake Superior at the head of the Great Lakes, it is a place of pulp mills and grain elevators, ocean freighters and endless railway trains. The people of Thunder Bay are daily spectators to the commercial bargain that is Canada, watching trains carrying Mustangs three-deep from east to west and freighters carrying No. 3 Northern from west to east. The surrounding countryside is the rugged, almost gloomy mixture of rock, wood and water celebrated in the impressionist paintings of the Group of Seven. The winters are long and cold. There are no Stanley Cups in Thunder Bay's history, but Fort William and Port Arthur were once pretty good hockey towns. In 1922, a team called the Fort William War Veterans won the Canadian junior hockey championship Memorial Cup. In 1948 the cup was won by the Port Arthur West End Bruins. In 1925, 1926, 1929 and 1939, the Port Arthur Bear Cats won the senior national championship Allan Cup. Those Bear Cat clubs, and their rivalries with the Fort William Seniors, the Red Lake Thunderers, the Geraldton Gold Miners and the Duluth Zephyrs, shortened the winters in the twin cities for almost 30 years. "People still talk about the playoff with Geraldton in '39," says Edgar Laprade, a Bear Cat star who went on to play for the New York Rangers from 1945 to 1955. "Hundreds of people came down to watch the series. They brought their gold trucks, their hard hats and their lanterns, and they tried to take over the town. In those days, senior hockey was as important to people as the NHL is today. All the games were sold out, wherever we played. I'm still remembered in Montreal more for the 1939 Allan Cup final against the Royals than for my days with the Rangers. And when we came home, the train stopped in Marathon, Terrace Bay, Schreiber and Red Rock, and they had bands out to greet us. Of course, the celebrations in Port Arthur lasted for days." All of Canada remembers Port Arthur stars like Laprade, Lorne Chabot, Danny Cox, Gaye Stewart, Gus Bodnar, Penti Lunde, Rudy Migay, Danny Lewicki, Alex Delvecchio and Bruce Gamble, all of whom went on to play in the NHL.

But around the Lakehead, and in the towns and cities where the Bear Cats played, people remember other Port Arthur stars, too — men like Bert Laprade, Jakie Nash, Hugh O'Leary, Walter Harbluck, Bones McCormack, Stan King, Gus Saxberg and Bobby Manahan. They were — and for many still are — Port Arthur's most popular hockey heroes because they were not just pictures on a television screen. People could talk to them on the street, watch them practise in the Port Arthur Arena. It was the immediacy of the Bear Cats that gave hockey vitality in Port Arthur. "In the 1930s," one fan recalls, "the NHL meant as much as the Cincinnati Redlegs. It was miles away." But hockey has been moribund in Thunder Bay since the late 1940s when the NHL started to pluck promising young hockey players out of small towns at a much earlier age. There is some junior hockey today, and out of love for the game, a group of local businessmen put up a few thousand dollars in 1970 to launch the Thunder Bay Twins in the semi-professional United States Senior Hockey League. But anyone who watches the game on television can tell the difference between good hockey and the hockey they play in the United States Senior Hockey League, and there are no lineups to see the Thunder Bay Twins. In Thunder Bay today the big sporting event of the year is not the Stanley Cup playoffs but the National Football League Superbowl, and the kids in Thunder Bay are as apt to idolize Joe Namath as Bobby Orr.

Hockey has become a television sport. The Canadian hockey fan has been exiled to his television set. Unless he lives in Vancouver, Edmonton, Winnipeg, Toronto, Ottawa, Montreal, Quebec City or Halifax, his choice is televised hockey or something on the order of the Thunder Bay Twins. And even if he lives in one of the cities with a professional team, he probably watches hockey on television just the same. The tickets are expensive and, besides, who can get them? The seating capacity at Maple Leaf Gardens is 16,314, and all but a few hundred of those seats are held by subscribers who pay as much as $600 for a pair of season's tickets. No one complains when the Gardens raises its prices because, as everybody knows, there is a waiting list with about 6,500 names on it. Those who have tickets consider themselves fortunate. People will them to their heirs. Since 1946, every Toronto Maple Leaf home game has been a sell-out, and the demand for tickets so far exceeds the supply that Morris Cohen, who makes $500 a week during the hockey season scalping tickets outside the Gardens' front door, can count on $25 for a $15.40 pair of reds — $40 if Boston is in town. So even in the cities where there is live professional hockey, only a privileged few get to see it.

The phenomenon of more people watching fewer games predates televised hockey. Long before the arrival of television, the owners of the NHL saw the advantages of operating the only game in town. But an arena has only so many seats, and building more costs money, whereas it costs no more to televise a game for 3 million fans than it does for 6 million. Television represented a means of increasing revenues (networks pay handsomely for the right to televise hockey) without significantly increasing costs. (Of course, as profits increased, players demanded more money — which put professional hockey more than ever beyond the reach of communities where it might otherwise have survived.) Television is the reason the NHL gave seven of the eight franchises it granted in the late Sixties to American rather than Canadian cities. There may have been other considerations, but what was uppermost in the minds of the NHL governors was the knowledge that expansion in Canada would not — could not — add many new fans to the 6

29

million Canadians who already followed the game on television. But in the United States, there was the potential of a new and much larger audience for televised hockey, and the anticipated revenue from that audience preoccupied the NHL. In 1963 NHL President Clarence Campbell told Arthur Daley of the *New York Times*: ". . . we will need a new box office. Only expansion will give it to us. No TV sponsor is too interested in financing on a national basis a program of big league hockey which ignores two thirds of the country [the United States] as far as member cities are concerned." On May 27, 1965, the NHL invited New York advertising and television executives to a reception at the Plaza Hotel, and showed them a colour videotape of a game between the Maple Leafs and the Canadiens. Campbell told them the league was not making a sales pitch. It just wanted to "demonstrate what is available in the field of hockey — the nature and quality of the product we have to offer". He admitted hockey was a problem for the American networks, because NHL games were played during evening prime time, but he said the problem would ultimately be solved.

In 1966, the NHL sold franchises to six American cities — Philadelphia, Pittsburgh, St. Louis, Minneapolis, Los Angeles and Oakland. Vancouver had applied and had been turned down, not because it could not support a team, but because the purpose of expansion was to open up new markets for televised hockey in the United States. In 1968 Vancouver tried to buy the ailing Oakland franchise but the NHL refused: it needed a team in the rich San Francisco Bay area to ensure its national television contract in the United States. Vancouver did get a franchise in 1969, as did Buffalo, but only because the Columbia Broadcasting System's Sunday afternoon hockey telecasts, begun in 1967, had been getting poor ratings. Vancouver and Buffalo would not bring the league more television revenue (they had been receiving Canadian telecasts for years), but with CBS losing interest and five of the six expansion clubs losing money, the prospect of two new franchises, self-sufficient at the box office, was very attractive. Eventually, televised hockey caught on in the United Sates. By the 1971-72 season the CBS *Game of the Week* had for the third year in a row attracted a large enough audience to turn a small but encouraging profit. So the NHL reverted to form. In 1971, franchises were granted to Atlanta and Long Island, and in 1972 to Kansas City and Washington, D.C.

If there was any doubt about American television's preferred position in the NHL's scheme of things, it was rudely dispelled on the evening of Saturday, May 4, 1968, when for the first time in 37 years, Saturday night was *not* hockey night in Canada. The Montreal Canadiens would normally have played a playoff game against St. Louis that night, but the game was postponed until Sunday afternoon to suit CBS. The NHL's contract with the American network stipulated that CBS must always be supplied with a Sunday afternoon game. Two weeks earlier, at a league meeting in New York's Gotham Hotel, the governors had decided that it would be impossible during the playoffs to follow a Saturday night game with another on Sunday afternoon. Faced, then, with a choice between *Hockey Night in Canada* or the CBS *Game of the Week,* they chose *Game of the Week,* and on Saturday, May 4, 10 million Canadian hockey fans had to make do with José Ferrer and Zsa Zsa Gabor in *Moulin Rouge.* Clarence Campbell had been as good as his word; ultimately the scheduling problem had been solved. Toronto sports columnist Ted Reeve was prompted to write:

Gather round chillun and observe the way
The N-H-L rules the C-A-H-A,
And while you're at it you can see as well
How the C-B-S rules the N-H-L.

Television has been disastrous for hockey, especially for the fans. It has been the means by which the NHL destroyed what little remained of the interest in amateur hockey that once filled arenas across the country. More than that, television has altered the quality of the spectacle itself. Jacques Plante, who has been watching hockey from an NHL goal-crease for 20 years, says he feels sorry for the fans watching the game on television. Most of the time, he says, all they see is a picture of a man carrying a puck.

Some sports work on television. Baseball does. So does football. Basketball does not. Soccer does not, and neither does hockey. Hockey does not make sense unless you can see the whole rink, so that even if you are following the puck — which is what the television camera does — your peripheral vision can pick up the winger on the other side of the ice making a move to break in behind the defence. The television camera misses that move, catching up with the winger only when he is taking a pass in the clear and moving in for a shot on goal. So watching hockey on television is a little like watching a movie from which critical scenes have been cut: in the end the white hats still beat the black hats, but you are never sure how or why. Televised hockey is a game of effects without causes. TV distorts the game, making the men who get the goals and the men who stop the goals larger than life, while reducing to insignificance the men who set up the plays and block the shots and pump up and down their wings all night keeping their checks out of trouble.

Television does awful things to the tempo of the game. The emotion of a hockey game, particularly a tight one, can change in the split second it takes to score a goal. Suddenly one team is up, the other down, and although that psychological advantage may last only a few minutes, perhaps a few seconds, it is often enough to change the game's course. But what if the instant a goal is scored or a team takes a penalty the game is interrupted for a commercial, as nowadays it nearly always is? That is what bothered Peter Gzowski a few years ago, when he wrote this letter to *The Globe and Mail*.

As your sports pages have already indicated, the Toronto-Montreal hockey game played Wednesday night at Maple Leaf Gardens was a stirring one. It must have made exciting television fare. I wonder, though, if the people who saw it on television realized how much of the game's edge was taken off by the catering of the men who presumably run hockey to the commercial sponsors of the telecast. I'm talking about the pauses in the flow of the play imposed for the sake of commercials. There were several occasions on Wednesday when a faceoff was delayed for no reason at all, other than to permit the ramming in of 60 full seconds of advertising. These pauses may be tolerable if you're watching the game at home, free, and want to go to the john or something. But at the Gardens they're a pain in what Scott Young would probably call one's a-dash-s. The worst case on Wednesday night occurred late in the third period. Until then, many of the highlights of the evening had been provided by the line of Keon, Ellis and Oliver, whose forechecking and artistic passing (artistic by Leaf standards, anyway) had gone a long way toward making up for the defence's habit of getting out of position. Now, with the score tied 4-4 and time running out, the line skated out for what appeared to be one last chance to beat the best hockey team in the world. And what happened? We got a pause. *The players skated around; the referees scratched their heads and the balloon of excitement that had been expanding all evening began to shrink in a chorus of impatient boos. Commercial. It would be argued, I suppose, that the Keon line, after working so hard all night, would have benefitted from the breather. But that, surely, wasn't the point. The point was that before the pause, the evening had a marvellous shape of its own, a dramatic construction of goal against goal, rush against rush, the kind of pace that puts a classic Leaf-Canadiens game high on the list of Toronto's theatrical attractions. And what the fans wanted to see at that time was a final confrontation, to see whether the gallant Keon and Ellis and Oliver could draw one last effort from their energy and pop in the winning goal.*

A hockey game is real in a way that most television shows are not, so the fan naturally assumes that a hockey telecast is journalism. He believes that the men in the broadcast booth are "reporters", that the men in the remote control unit parked behind the arena are "editors", and that together they are "covering" the game as a television news team would cover a political convention. He is wrong. And that is another indignity television has inflicted on hockey: it has turned it into a show. Since 1931, when a Maple Leaf game was first broadcast over a Toronto radio station, MacLaren Advertising Company Ltd. has owned exclusive broadcasting rights in Maple Leaf Gardens. MacLaren's is the largest agency in the country, and *Hockey Night in Canada* is one of its properties. When they roll the *Hockey Night in Canada* credits and the announcer says, "This has been a CBC [or

CTV] presentation", it is only half true. MacLaren's buys time on the two networks, CBC on Saturday nights, CTV on Wednesday nights. The technical work is done by personnel provided by the networks' Toronto affiliates, CBLT on Saturday nights and CFTO on Wednesday nights. But the producers, the commentators, the interviewers — the people who give the telecasts their character — are under contract not to the networks, but to MacLaren Advertising Company Ltd. And to MacLaren's, *Hockey Night in Canada* is a vehicle to sell gasoline, automobiles, loans and beer. Its first concern is not the fan, nor the game, but the sponsor. Which makes happy collaborators out of all of them: MacLaren's, which is selling advertising time; its clients, who are selling their products; and the NHL, which is selling itself. *Hockey Night in Canada* is less a report of an event than an advertisement for one. The commentary is upbeat, the interviews bland. Seldom is heard a discouraging word, and MacLaren's likes it that way.

Shortly after he began writing a sport column in *The Globe and Mail* in 1963, Dick Beddoes was in Detroit covering a playoff game between the Leafs and the Red Wings. *Hockey Night in Canada* asked him to appear as a between-periods guest. That afternoon, chatting in the lobby of the Leland hotel, George Retzlaff, the director, had told him, "I'm going to make a big man out of you." Beddoes went on that night and several times after, but as it became apparent that he had a tendency to call a bad game a bad game he didn't get any more invitations. "It's the hacks who get the work on *Hockey Night in Canada*," says Beddoes, "people who don't tell you what's going on. People with a magnificent grasp of the obvious. And that's not what the fans want. They know it's a tough game, a hard game. They've played it, their kids play it, they've known about it from the cradle. And you insult their intelligence when you don't tell them exactly who hit whom." The list of people *persona non grata* on *Hockey Night in Canada* at one point included even Scotty Morrison, the NHL's referee-in-chief. In January, 1969, Leaf defenceman Jim Dorey accused referee John Ashley of calling him "pretty boy" and "bright eyes" during a game in Boston. The story got into the papers. A few days later, Morrison was asked to appear on a Wednesday night *Hockey Night in Canada* telecast. He was to go on just before the start of the game with Brian McFarlane. "Before I went on," says Morrison, "I had a discussion with John and he emphatically denied that he had said those things, and I believed him." Morrison told McFarlane and a national television audience that Ashley had been wrongly accused. Maple Leaf Gardens' contract with MacLaren's gives the Leafs the right to veto anyone's appearance on *Hockey Night in Canada* when it originates in Toronto. Punch Imlach, the Leafs' coach and general manager, had used this prerogative to bar appearances by ex-Leafs Andy Bathgate, Bert Olmstead and Billy Harris, and former Leaf trainer Bob Haggert. Now he turned on Morrison. "I don't need him [Morrison] making out one of my players is a liar," said Imlach. And with that, he announced that Morrison would never appear on *Hockey Night in Canada* again.

The quality of American hockey telecasts is just as bad. Up until the 1972-73 season, NHL hockey was brought to national television audiences in the United States by CBS (NBC took over in 1972), and the CBS *Game of the Week* promoted the NHL more blatantly than *Hockey Night in Canada*. When *Game of the Week* went on the air, Don V. Ruck, the NHL's vice-president in charge of public relations, was in the control booth giving the cues for three 30-second commercials and one 60-second commercial every period. (The linesmen were equipped with a transistor device that would buzz when a commercial was in progress.) Presumably Ruck had something to say about other aspects of the telecasts as well, because the NHL's contract with CBS gave it power of approval over the broadcasters and commentators on the programme. The attitude towards hockey Ruck represented, sitting there in the CBS control booth, was perhaps best illustrated by a comment he made in an interview with a New York reporter in 1968. Asked if *Game of the Week* would continue to zero in its cameras on fights, Ruck replied: "We don't care to make a special programme out of a riot, but some games have been of the kind where I felt as if I'd like to go out and start some fights."

Television has brought NHL hockey to millions of fans who would otherwise have gone without, but what does that mean? Are they better off in their living rooms watching NHL hockey on television than they would be in the local arena watching a good amateur game? Ten years ago, it would have been possible to argue that the quality of NHL hockey was so superior to anything a fan might see in a community arena that televised hockey, with all its limitations, was a blessing. But not today. The price for television was expansion, and expansion has done more damage to the game than anything else.

Clarence Campbell has said all along, as if admitting it made it all right, that "you can't take half a bottle of whisky and fill it with water and still have the same drink". What the NHL did in fact was take a full bottle of whisky and by adding water make two. In the expansion of 1966, about 120 new players were brought into the league — old pros who would otherwise have been forced to retire (in 1960, Johnny Bower was the only player in the league to have reached the age of 35; today there are 26), and rookies who would otherwise never have made the NHL. Then, in the expansion of 1969, it added more water, and in the expansion of 1972, still more water, so that, where there was one bottle of whisky in 1966, today there are almost three. By 1980, when the league expects to have 24 franchises, there will be four. Maybe we could have developed a tolerance for whisky with water if it had been watered down with care, but the NHL was sloppy. Expansion is commonplace in modern professional sport, but it is usually undertaken in a way that puts the new teams on a nearly equal footing with the old. In big league baseball, football and basketball, the strong teams are invariably the expansion teams — the New York Mets, Houston Astros and Oakland Athletics in baseball; the New York Jets, Kansas City Chiefs and Dallas Cowboys in football; the Milwaukee Bucks in basketball. It is obvious: the only way to keep the fans interested is to ensure that on any given day any team is liable to beat any other. And the only way to make that happen is to give the weakest teams a shot at the best new players. So what did the NHL do? It allowed the old teams to protect their best players, leaving the expansion clubs with mostly has-beens and also-rans. And worse than that, it allowed the expansion clubs to trade away their draft choices in exchange for players they needed and could not otherwise get. Thus, in 1971, the Montreal Canadiens traded Ralph Backstrom to the Los Angeles Kings and Gordon Labossiere to the Minnesota North Stars, in an effort to ensure the last place finish of the California Seals. Montreal owned the Seals' first draft choice, which, when the Seals finished last, gave the Canadiens first crack at Guy Lafleur in the junior amateur draft. The expansion franchises started out weak and, taken as a group, have grown steadily weaker. Even Campbell is concerned. In a confidential report to the NHL governors at the beginning of the 1971-72 season, he described the imbalance between the new and old franchises as "the league's number one problem". He pointed out that at the end of the 1970-71 season, Boston, in first place in the East Division, finished 66 points ahead of last place Detroit. In the West Division, 62 points separated first place Chicago and last place California. In the 1971-72 season, 71 points separated Boston and Vancouver in the East Division, 58 points separated Chicago and Los Angeles in the West. So instead of watering down one bottle of whisky to make nearly three, the NHL has set before the fans one bottle of slightly diluted whisky and two bottles of water smelling faintly of alcohol.

On most nights, it is sheer nostalgia to call it hockey. Exaggeration? Not so long ago, it was the exceptional NHL player who scored 20 goals a season. In 1971-72, 62 players, eight of them Boston Bruins, scored 20 goals. One of them was Vic Hadfield, an 11-year veteran with the New York Rangers. In the best of his six seasons with the Rangers before expansion, Hadfield scored 18 goals. In the 1971-72 season he scored 50. John McKenzie scored 67 goals in 343 pre-expansion games in the NHL. In 348 games after expansion he scored 139. In his rookie year with the Buffalo Sabres, Richard Martin scored 44 goals. Rookies did not develop quite that quickly in the pre-expansion NHL. Frank Mahovlich, the league's outstanding rookie in 1957-58, scored 20 goals, seven more than runner-up Bobby Hull. The following season, Ralph Backstrom was the highest scoring rookie with 18 goals. Gordie Howe scored seven goals in his rookie year, as did Yvan Cournoyer. Phil Esposito scored three. Sure, the style of the game has changed; it is more offensive, so naturally, there are more goals. But it is more offensive because of the disparities created by expansion. When the Boston Bruins play the California Seals, the forwards can afford to forget about defensive hockey and concentrate on scoring goals. If Boston played a defensive game, California would be lucky to get a shot on net. If scoring goals were all it took to make hockey exciting, we would have no cause for complaint. But it is not. Maybe they cannot tell the difference in Oakland and all the other American towns and cities where hockey has only recently joined baseball, football and basketball as one of the things that go better with Coca-Cola, but there are goals and there are *goals*. Since expansion, more goals are being scored on shots fired through a maze of legs from the blueline. Fewer goals are the culmination of great rushes, well-executed passing plays, skating and stickhandling and the other fine points of the hockey player's art. But then art is less and less a part of the game today. The typical NHL game is characterized by offensive rushes in which the puck carrier simply skates over the centre redline and dumps it into the corner. If, in the ensuing scramble, a player on the attacking team gets possession, he will usually drop the puck back to a defenceman at the blueline for a slapshot. If a player on the defending team comes up with the puck, he will usually hold it against the boards for a faceoff. He could try to carry the puck out, but there are not many players in the league today who can stickhandle through heavy traffic. This dump-the-puck-into-the-corner-and-see-what-happens continues back and forth, up and down the ice, until one of the defencemen gets away a shot from the point that hits the goalie on the pads and drops to his feet where some 20-goal-a-year man bangs it in. All the while, interference, holding, boarding and a variety of other fouls will go unnoticed, or at least unacknowledged, by the referee. Players

rent effect of a $100 fine on a hockey player earning $45,000 a year is marginal — even if he pays it himself. And not by automatically expelling the third man into a fight. The third-man rule has eliminated the bench-emptying brawls, it is true, but it still leaves any two players free to fight, knowing that the only punishment they will receive is a penalty. Clarence Campbell and the governors of the NHL know that fines and the third-man rule will not eliminate fights. And that is precisely why they impose them. It permits them to *seem* to be doing something to "stamp out this kind of stuff" while in fact doing nothing at all. It is sometimes argued that fighting is integral to hockey. Scotty Morrison, the NHL's referee-in-chief, subscribes to this point of view. In December, 1971, he told a reporter:

Many people have pointed out that there is more body contact in football than hockey, but players who engage in football fights are automatically ejected from the game. The difference in the rules is in the difference of the two games. Collisions in football are constant and relatively consistent; linemen are at each other throughout the game and their aggressiveness is channelled in direct confrontations. The pace of hockey makes it a much more mobile sport, a game in which players sideswipe each other rather than crash headlong. A flying elbow in the face may provoke instant retaliation with two players dropping their sticks and gloves and fighting. I view this as entirely more acceptable than a player retaliating by slashing with his stick. If there was a rule which automatically ejected a player for fighting, there would be a definite increase in slashing, a dangerous practice and one I personally detest. The hockey stick can become a deadly weapon by its very shape and the strength of the player swinging it.

42

Tom Watt, coach of the University of Toronto Blues, and one of the country's most knowledgeable students of the game, disagrees. "Hockey no more leads to fighting than playing cards leads to gambling," he says. "There's opportunity for fighting in hockey, that's all." Anyone who has played soccer knows that fighting — and flagrant slashing, too — could be eliminated from hockey by a strictly enforced, automatic suspension rule. And cheap violence — the elbowing, cross-checking, charging and kneeing that raise the temperature of a game to the ignition point — could be eliminated if a penalized team were denied the freedom to ice the puck. Why should a team that is supposedly being punished for breaking the rules be given an advantage at the same time? In 1956, the NHL compounded the hypocrisy by allowing the penalized player to return to the ice after one goal was scored. The Montreal Canadiens' power play with Doug Harvey, Bernie Geoffrion, Jean Beliveau, Bert Olmstead and Maurice Richard was so explosive that during a two-minute penalty it could score several goals.

The institutionalized violence so common in the NHL today insults the fans. Sure they enjoy it, some more than others, but that does not mean they would not prefer displays of the athletic skill for which it is so cynically substituted. The fans are being used. What the owners of the NHL are saying is: "It doesn't matter whether we give the suckers a good hockey game as long as we give them a fight."

Unfortunately, the NHL sets the style for all hockey in Canada. The undesirable characteristics of the professional game are emulated in neighbourhood rinks and arenas, where hockey is *not* a business. Ten years ago, you could watch a peewee game anywhere in Canada and see nothing more violent than an innocent trip. Today, kids the same age are running at one another. The Wayne Cashmans and

Rosaire Paiements are not disgraced for their quick-fisted approach to the game; they are rewarded for it. Derek Sanderson would never have received the enormous public recognition he now enjoys were it not for his record as a brawler. (In 1965 Sanderson and Paiement were leading figures in a bloody Memorial Cup series between the Niagara Falls Flyers and the Edmonton Oil Kings.) Crack a few heads, bloody a few noses and the next thing you know the newspapers are writing stories about you, the fans are taking notice, and the guy who pays your salary (and who does not care why the fans come to see you, so long as they come) is patting you on the back and slipping you a bonus. Television does not help. "When a guy gets a penalty the cameras zoom in on him," observes Terry O'Malley, who played hockey with the St. Catharines Teepees and later the Harvard Crimsons. "And then we see the penalty in slow motion. And then we see him skate to the penalty box, swearing all the way, telling the referee what a dummy he is. And then we get a super of his name. It costs a lot of money to buy 30 seconds on *Hockey Night in Canada,* and you get a lot of viewers, so if that guy gets two penalties in a night he's got a campaign going." None of this is lost on kids. They see dirty play rewarded so they assume it is one of the skills of the game, like skating and stickhandling. If you cannot skate very well and if the puck seems to get away from you all the time, maybe you reach the same conclusion Allan Globensky came to a few years ago. Globensky was a 19-year-old defenceman with the Montreal Junior Canadiens, an unspeakably bad hockey player, but the acknowledged heavyweight champion of the Ontario Hockey Association Junior "A". "I would never have made this team," he admitted one day, "if it weren't for my fighting ability." Kids are the real victims of what the NHL has done to the game of hockey, because they have never known anything better. On Sunday afternoons they jam Maple Leaf Gardens to cheer the Toronto Marlboros of the OHA Junior "A". A seat costs as little as 75 cents. What takes place on the ice is a parody of the style of hockey that is played in the Gardens the night before, obviously derivative but exaggerated, more routinely and lustily violent. The Marlboros once played a game against the Oshawa Generals in which seven players had to be helped from the ice. A few years ago one of the most popular Marlboros was a big defenceman named Steve Durbano whose special talent was dirty checks. The kids ate it up. "Hit him again Durbano, he's still breathing," they would yell. "Kill the bum." And then, to each other approvingly, "Did you see that Durbano? He's an animal." The kids do not know that once there was a game that offered something more exciting than the pathetic spectacle of grown men slashing each other with hockey sticks. If they did, they would probably feel about hockey today the way Morley Callaghan does:

When I was a kid my friends and I would stand for hours outside Toronto's old Mutual Street Arena to get tickets for a hockey game. That was when the old St. Patricks team was playing in Toronto. When I was 12 every hockey player was a hero to me. Hockey players aren't my heroes anymore, but at that time they took in everybody and everybody's brother. I used to go to hockey games all the time about 12 years ago. Now I only watch the Stanley Cup games on TV. You grow up with hockey and there are people you follow all along, but during this business of NHL expansion I just lost interest. I can't whip up the slightest bit of interest in the California Seals. And even though I know Jack Kent Cooke, I don't give a darn about his Los Angeles Kings. It's sort of another world now. It has no connection with me anymore. The personal attachment seems to be gone. I remember one time my wife and I were visiting Dink Carroll, the sports columnist of the Montreal Gazette, *and he'd arranged for us to go to a game at the Forum on Saturday night. Tickets were hard to get, but we had something else we wanted to do, and he was absolutely astonished, flabbergasted, in fact he was downright shocked that we would rather do something else than go to a hockey game. It's a funny thing, but hockey in this country used to be almost a religion.*

The Child Buyers

Grey is the forelock now of the Irishman,
stick-handler of my roaring Twenties birthright,
F. Scott Fitzgerald of the sporting world,
(and, between games, father to me).

My beautiful brain-washed Canadian sons
are bringing in the whole neighbourhood
to see the old pro alive,
the all-round right-wing Maple Leaf god,
Adonis of an arena now crumbled
and fallen into the cannibal maw of mobs.

The boys, crowding in at the door,
surround him with a fiery ring of worship,
envying his eyebrows,
thick with scars inflicted by the high sticking
of old idols, Clancy, Morenz, Horner —

(and, my god, one of them is standing at attention!)

When I was their age, unholily dreamful,
full of the same power of innocence,
I saw crowds pick him up and carry him away,
policemen trampled down,

hysterical women following their infatuation
to the barricaded hotel-room doors,
crying in the corridors
their need for illusion;

and I remember the millionaires who courted him
whose money had not bought them youth
and the golden skates of fame;
one of them especially used to invite him
into his suite at the Royal York for an oyster feed,
then ordered up by phone,
crustaceans, wine, stove, pans, chef and all;
another used to send him every Christmas
suitably engraved silver dishes
which my mother never used;

I remember my father, too, in the headlines,
on the gum cards, in the rotogravure,
and how, in the pasture, there was nothing
to charge but shadows and, in the dark beyond night,
bright enormous butterflies crossing the moon
of his disenchanted vision; I heard him cry out to them
in another room but they stayed in his eyes
until we were all well-marked by the days
of his going down into ruin.

Wrinkled now is the brow of my all-star father
standing in the doorway
of his grandchildren generation
who yet must learn,
in smaller forums and with less limelight,
how heroes are really made.

—Grey is the Forelock Now of the Irishman, *by Joan Finnigan*

On May 19, 1971 the fate of 144 16-year-old hockey players was decided at the Rock Haven Motel in Peterborough where the Ontario Hockey Association held its annual midget draft. Each of the OHA's 10 junior teams selected about 15 players to invite to their training camps in the fall. For each boy they drafted they paid the midget teams between $300 and $400. The OHA midget draft was instituted in 1964, and it has been successful in dividing talent evenly throughout the league and thereby providing more exciting hockey. So much so that in 1971-72 the league took in more than $2 million at the box office. But sometimes a boy does not want to play for the team that drafts him. Such a boy was Stuart Towers, who lived in Clarkson, Ontario, and who was drafted in 1971 by the Peterborough Petes. It took eight months for the Petes, the Toronto Marlboros and the Ottawa '67s (for whom Towers eventually played) to work out a deal satisfactory to Towers and his father, and in the interval he did not play hockey. If a deal had not been made, he could have sat out his junior years at home and, in the words of one junior "A" owner, stayed there "until he rots".

Child buying is the most degrading consequence of the commercialization of hockey. For thousands of Canadian boys, and for as long as anyone can remember, it has meant learning to become a mercenary, to fight someone else's battles, to bolster someone else's ego, to line someone else's pocket. It has meant leaving home and quitting school to take up a life of boarding houses, early marriages, too much booze, all-night bus rides, and wasted time in pool halls and empty arenas. An adolescence of brief explosions of excitement and eternities of loneliness. Perhaps these boys benefit materially, but in the exchange they relinquish their control over hockey and, much more important, their own lives. That is one of the reasons Canadian hockey has ceased to be a sport. At almost every level, it is played primarily for the benefit of the men who put up the cash — the sponsors, the junior team operators, the 16 owners of the National Hockey League — and only indirectly for the players themselves.

Child buying is no secret. In 1971, the following story was published in the sports pages of the *Toronto Star:*

Cedar Hill peewees of the Metropolitan Toronto Hockey League, winners of the Quebec peewee tournament last year and MTHL finalists, haven't won in their 39 games this season, a dismal turnabout to say the least.

But, to Cedar Hill Association president Bob McDowell, not all surprising.

"We were raped," he said simply.

"There were a number of reasons why the team has done so poorly, but mainly it's been the result of what I term 'parasite' clubs, which carry out wholesale raids to strengthen their teams."

Of 60 top peewee and atom players last year, only seven remain in the Cedar Hill organization.

"I have a letter from the Don Valley organization sent to the father of a 7-year-old and it's enough to make me sick," said McDowell.

"It promises equipment to the boy if he makes their team, tickets to all Marlboro Junior A league and playoff games, admission to a Leafs' practice, and the promise of a trip which would be 'the highlight of the boy's minor hockey career.'

"This letter was followed up by a personal visit, in which the equipment was all laid out for the boy to see, and the

promise of a trip to Sweden. That was later changed to Finland."

Stories like that have appeared in newspapers across the country. Child buying has been documented by the federal government and the Alberta government, condemned by the Synod of the Anglican Church and the United Church *Observer*. The federal government is now studying it again. But still the practice continues. It is deplorable, and yet it is accepted. It is accepted by the boys themselves. A few years ago the sports editor at the *Edmonton Journal* asked the members of the Edmonton Junior Oil Kings, who were bound by contract to the Detroit Red Wings, whether they had any objections. They told him they did not. "If this is slavery," said one, "let's have a lot more of it." It is accepted by parents, although, as Clarence Campbell once told the *Toronto Star,* they are often given financial inducements. The idea that hockey is a means to an end — that is how Alan Eagleson, the executive director of the NHL Players' Association, puts it — is accepted by nearly everyone. It is so pervasive that it blinds us to the harm it does to boys and to the game itself.

Hockey should be fun, a game played for the excitement and satisfaction it brings players *while they are playing it* and the delight it brings spectators *while they are watching it.* The joy of hockey is of the moment. That is why five-year-olds play it all day on vacant parking lots. It is the reason retired NHLers like Darryl Sly, Gerry McNamara and Henry Monteith, now playing in the Senior OHA, refuse to give it up. However, too much Canadian hockey is played not for the joy of the moment but for the demands of a parent, the reputation of a house league organizer or the recognition of a pro scout. Too often the shape of the game is determined by outsiders. "Kids will play road hockey all day long and there'll never be a fight," observes Andy Higgins, who teaches physical education at the University of Toronto. "But if an adult is watching or if you give them sweaters and shoulder pads and put them in a rink with a referee there'll often be trouble. Because then they're not *playing*. They're expected to win." Hockey ceases to be *playing* when it becomes solely a question of winning and — worse — of winning at all cost. It means learning how to fight. Not long ago a peewee coach was overheard shouting at his players, "Let there be blood on *their* sweaters." In 1970 the Metropolitan Hockey League advised teams to stop shaking hands at the completion of a game because it was precipitating post-game fights. This kind of hockey is not fun, it is work. It does not take *all* the pleasure out of the game — that would be impossible — but it has led thousands of boys to write hockey off. Those it does not turn off it turns into little businessmen.

The NHL began extending its tentacles into community hockey in the late 1920s. To ensure a steady supply of players, the pro clubs would pay an amateur a retainer, give him a job or keep him in school in return for a promise that if he turned pro he would sign with no other team. Almost from the day he purchased the Toronto St. Pats in 1926, Conn Smythe brought talented juniors to Toronto, paying their tuition at St. Michael's College so they could play hockey for St. Mike's or the Marlboros. By the end of the Second World War, the NHL's need for young players was so great that clubs began sponsoring junior teams outright, turning them into development teams recruited from all over Canada. The Canadiens had the Junior Canadiens, the Rangers the Guelph Biltmores, the Boston Bruins the Barrie Flyers and Estevan Bruins, the Chicago Black Hawks the St. Catharines Teepees, and so on. By 1967, at the height of the sponsorship system, 27 professional teams in North America, all but five of which were located in the United States, owned 50 Canadian junior teams. The system was sanctioned by the NHL-CAHA agreements of 1947 and 1958, and it gave the pros control over virtually every amateur player in the country. "The money barons of the NHL have relegated Canada to the role of a gigantic hockey slave farm," the CAHA's full-time secretary manager, Gordon Juckes, told the Western Canada Senior Hockey League in 1966. "We are now to be only the Gold Coast of hockey." Before the Second World War, the CAHA had been completely independent of the NHL. In fact, its flourishing senior community leagues had competed with the NHL for players. But five years of war had seriously weakened the community leagues, and the CAHA thought it needed the NHL's money to stay afloat. In order to get that money the CAHA signed over amateur hockey to the NHL. The 1947 and 1958 agreements were the articles of surrender. Sponsorship was the most sophisticated system of apprentice control ever devised by a professional sport. Its genius was the way it made the CAHA an active partner in the development of a country-wide NHL farm system. The CAHA eventually came to believe — and to teach thousands of young players whose activity it regulated— that what was good for the NHL was good for hockey.

The CAHA gave the NHL control over many more players than those whose bills it actually paid. While the NHL limited each of its teams to sponsoring "not more than three officially affiliated teams of midget category or higher," a total of not more than 60 players, the CAHA enabled the professional clubs to control hundreds of players by defining a "club" as consisting of a senior, intermediate, junior "A," junior "B" or juvenile, midget, and bantam teams, and all the "house league" players affiliated with those teams. Thus, if an NHL team controlled the town's junior "A" team, it controlled every registered player in town. The CAHA even provided the form by which the amateur player signed away his future. All amateur players were — and still are — required to sign a CAHA registration card. One part is used by the player's team, recording his desire to play for that team, and the other part is kept on file by the CAHA. In the days of sponsorship there was a third part which, when signed, bound the player for life to whatever NHL club happened to sponsor the junior team in his area. The third part was sent to the NHL's central registry in Montreal. As a result, every boy in Fredericton grew up knowing he was "Black Hawk property", every boy in Winnipeg "belonged" to the Boston Bruins.

Not every boy started out playing for one of the "chains" — there were some cities where the NHL did not sponsor hockey. And in certain circumstances, say when a boy's family moved from one town to another or when he enrolled in college, a player was entitled to his release. The NHL covered these loopholes with seven lists of players each team regarded as its exclusive property: the Players' Reserve List, the Goal Keepers' Reserve List, the Voluntarily Retired List, the Negotiation List, the Sponsorship List, the Inactive List, and the A, B, and C Tryout Forms. If an NHL team discovered a promising player outside its chain it simply placed him on its Negotiation List (a particularly repugnant practice, because a boy could be listed without his or his parents' permission). If a player moved from one city to another, from Moose Jaw, say, to Ottawa, the Chicago Black Hawks, which sponsored the Moose Jaw chain, could put him on their Sponsorship List, preventing him from playing for any team other than the St. Catharines Teepees or the Dixie Beehives, the teams Chicago sponsored in Ontario. If a player entered university, the NHL club that sponsored his junior hockey would place him on its Inactive List so he could never become a "free agent" (Steve Monteith, who played junior hockey in the Red Wing chain in Stratford, Ontario, remained "Detroit property" through six years at the University of Toronto). As if the lists were not enough, in 1962 the NHL instituted — over the protest of the CAHA — an amateur draft enabling each team to draft any two junior players no matter whose property they were. One advantage of owning players is that you can sell them. According to the Hockey Study Committee of the National Advisory Council on Fitness and Amateur Sport, the releases of boys as young as 14 were regularly bought and traded. Sometimes the pros even sold amateur players to amateur clubs. In 1955, the Kitchener-Waterloo Dutchmen had to pay the Toronto Maple Leafs $1,000 for the "rights" to Jack Mackenzie, a brilliant forward who did not want to play professional hockey. He had once signed a Leaf Tryout Form and was therefore Toronto property. In 1957 Clarence Campbell told a United States Senate subcommittee that "the sponsored teams provide 95 per cent of the players who find their way onto the rosters of professional clubs". Small wonder.

Sponsorship gave the NHL the run of amateur hockey in Canada. NHL clubs shuttled sponsored players from one part of the country to another to strengthen their junior teams. Bobby Hull, for instance, was sent to Dresden when he was 13, then to Ingersoll and then to St. Catharines. The Hockey Study Committee reported that 104 province-to-province transfers were made in 1965-66, 38 of them involving boys under 18 years of age. Most of these transfers took boys from their homes in the North and the West and brought them to Ontario to play in the OHA Junior "A," a practice that accounts for the league's dominance of postwar Memorial Cup championships (since 1945 the West has won the cup only six times). Although the transfers disrupted the quality of junior competition elsewhere in Canada, the CAHA was powerless to stop them. Under its agreement with the NHL it could not toughen the regulations for province-to-province transfers without the NHL's prior permission.

The sponsorship system came to an end in 1966. That was the year the NHL expanded from six to 12 teams, granting new franchises in six American cities: Philadelphia, Pittsburgh, Minnesota, St. Louis, Los Angeles and Oakland. The owners of the six old clubs — Toronto, Montreal, Boston, New York, Detroit and Chicago — realized that to retain their junior "chains" would give them so great an advantage that the six new clubs could not compete — on the ice or at the box office. The new teams had to be given access to the best graduating junior players, so in 1967 the NHL replaced the sponsorship system with today's universal junior draft. The draft did not require the NHL to relinquish any of its control over amateur hockey. It merely changed the rules by which the NHL owners divide the spoils. The NHL still determines the rules under which the CAHA plays, so that young players learn not hockey but NHL hockey. The NHL still controls the age at which juniors must turn pro. In its 1967 agreement with the NHL the CAHA undertook to lower the age limit of junior hockey from 21 to 20, despite the objection of regional hockey associations representing 200,000 of the 265,000 registered amateur players. The change gave the NHL, then desperate for players because of expansion, access to top juniors a year earlier, but it weakened junior hockey. It accelerated the exodus of young players to American colleges where they could continue to play beyond the age of 20 without turning pro. The NHL still controls the CAHA-NHL development committee, which approves all payments to CAHA leagues from the funds collected from the universal junior draft. The NHL's agreement with the CAHA stipulates that if the NHL is not satisfied with the number or calibre of players graduating from junior hockey, the CAHA must undertake a program of accelerated player development. If that fails, as Clarence Campbell has threatened more than once, the NHL is prepared to revert to sponsorship. Little wonder the Hockey Study Committee concluded that "the amateur and autonomous status of the CAHA is even more in question now [1967] than it was under the 1958 agreement". The only real difference between the sponsorship system and the universal draft, was that now the NHL was no longer directly involved. The child buying continued as it had before and with the same results, but now the buying and trading was carried out by the junior, juvenile, midget and bantam team operators themselves (and sometimes, as in the case of Cedar Hill, the peewees, atom and tyke team operators, too). The NHL still ran the show, but thanks to the CAHA, someone else now pulled the strings.

The practice of plucking young boys away from their families to play hockey somewhere else continues. In 1967 Guy Lafleur left his home in Thurso, a small lumbering town about 25 miles from Ottawa, to play for the Remparts in Québec. He was 15. Junior scouts are already interested in Brantford star Wayne Gretzky, who is only 12. There are thousands of volunteer coaches and organizers involved in the staging of kids' hockey all across the country, juggling schedules, driving kids to practices, paying out good money for ice time, gas, insurance, referees and equipment. A few of them have become a direct party to the NHL apprenticeship system. The others are being used.

Apologists for the NHL will tell you that child buying is all to the benefit of the children, that the players who make it as far as the NHL are paid a great deal of money to play hockey, more perhaps than they could have hoped to make in any other career. "If hockey players are slaves," the *Montreal Star's* John Robertson has written, "then they rattle their chains all the way to the bank." *The Globe and Mail's* Gord Walker puts it this way: "It will be difficult indeed to attack a business where the hired hands average better than $30,000 a year in salary and benefits, but somebody will try." NHL salaries are high, and competition from the new World Hockey Association has driven them higher — about 35 per cent higher, according to Alan Eagleson. NHL pensions are good, too. But let us not forget that only recently have the owners been willing to share their profits with the players. In 1947 the players asked the NHL to contribute to a pension fund. The owners refused, setting up instead the annual NHL All-Star Game with two-thirds of the gross proceeds going to players' pensions. Ten years later, Ted Lindsay, Doug Harvey, Jim Thomson and a few others formed the Players' Association and had to go to the Ontario Labour Relations Board before the NHL would agree to a minimum salary of $7,000 a year and a larger share of playoff money. The association's leaders — or "ringleaders" as the owners called them — were punished, Lindsay, Thomson, Tod Sloan, Bert Olmstead and Fern Flaman being shipped off to other teams. "I find it very difficult to imagine," said Conn Smythe, "that the captain of my club [Thomson] should find time during the hockey season to influence youngsters to join an association that has no specific plans to benefit or improve hockey." The Players' Association collapsed. Only after the Teamsters threatened to organize the NHL in 1966 did the league agree in 1967 to negotiate with Eagleson's NHL Players' Association. It is a good company union. "Players will have to learn that owners have to make profits, too," Eagleson has said. Nothing to upset the business of hockey. In fact, Eagleson has so totally accepted the NHL way of doing business that he is a popular choice as the successor to Clarence Campbell — that is, if he does not become a team owner first.

The NHL pays good money, but that is all it does. The working conditions in the NHL are nearly barbaric. Players are still subject to the arbitrary discipline of the owners and the league and can be fined at any time for what a sulking coach calls "indifferent play". They are still separated from their families during playoffs because of the medieval belief that only monasticism makes machos out of the men. (Conn Smythe once demoted Leaf centre Johnny McCormack because he got married during the season without Smythe's permission.) And they are still bound to the NHL for life by what is known as the reserve clause in the standard player's contract. A Canadian football player becomes a free agent a year after his contract expires; a British soccer player can demand to be traded; but a Canadian hockey player is stuck. To forestall the WHA's attempts to have the reserve clause thrown out of the courts — the new league's success in holding on to players like Derek Sanderson and Bobby Hull depends upon its ability to have the reserve clause declared unconstitutional — the NHL has agreed to allow any player who is not offered a contract by

August 10 of any year to bargain with any other team. Which means that now the reserve clause applies only to players the NHL wants to keep. The same provisions apply in the minor professional leagues, but because the NHL regards them as only development leagues there is a limit to the number of years a player can remain in them. All teams in the American Hockey League must play two rookies a year and not more than five players over 25. In 1970, the Springfield Indians were fined $1,000 for having too many players over the age of 25. Some job security. And then there is the length of the NHL schedule. "No athlete," says Tom Watt, coach of the University of Toronto hockey team, "can get up physically and mentally for a 78-game schedule." Particularly when the schedule involves travelling close to 100,000 miles a year (before expansion it was about 30,000). The marvel of players like Bobby Orr, Frank Mahovlich and Ken Dryden is that, with the 78-game schedule and all the travelling, they play good hockey at all. They spend too much energy getting on and off buses and planes, moving from one hotel room to the next and out of one time zone into another to have much enthusiasm left for hockey. "Hockey's no picnic," Ron Ellis admitted a few years ago. "I'm certainly not going to be playing when I'm 40. I may not play much longer at all. It's a tough way to make a living."

Money is important to the players because it is their only hedge against the day when an injury or advancing years forces them to retire. Most of them have been denied an opportunity to prepare for any career other than hockey. The owners and general managers of the NHL have traditionally seen education as an enemy of hockey. The late Stafford Smythe once berated Western League all-star Bill MacFarland for "that nonsense of going to college. He could have been a 10-year man with the Leafs. Instead, he's a minor leaguer and nobody's ever heard of him. That's what a college education got him." Today MacFarland is president of the Western Hockey League. In the spring of 1969, Jack McMaster of the Maple Leaf Gardens public relations staff wrote the following words of advice to young hockey players in the Marlboros' official programme:

For every boy capable of playing junior hockey in Canada, at some point he is going to have to make the big decision — to aim his sights at the National Hockey League, at Canada's National Team or towards College hockey in the United States. The record speaks for itself. Any boy who wants to be a professional hockey player should keep his sights firmly fixed on the NHL without ever waivering [sic] or diverting for, once diverted, he might never get back on the track again. The concept for our National Team has had a fair test. But this latest series with the Russian Nationals has laid bare the inadequacies of Canada's team. And what about the players? The NHL Minnesota North Stars took seven players from last year's National Squad to their training camp last fall and only one player, Danny O'Shea, has made a favourable impression. In today's world, education is a must. Hence the thought and appeal of College hockey. However, the dedicated individual can combine both professional hockey and an education. Dick Duff of the Montreal Canadiens and Bob Pulford of the Maple Leafs are shining examples of this. They both earned college degrees while playing in the NHL. Many other professional players are doing the same thing. On the other hand, look at the number of highly rated juniors over the years who have gone down to College and have disappeared from the hockey scene altogether. Hockey scouts report that if they didn't recognize the boy's name in the college program, they would never have been able to pick him out on the ice. The choice is, of course, up to the individual. However, if a player has any aspirations at all of making the NHL, he should set his sights and not falter. It could be one of the most rewarding decisions he ever made.

The tough junior "A" schedule makes it almost impossible for even those players who want to attend school to do so. As Ron Ellis has said: "Most professional hockey players sacrifice most of their youth. All they do is go to school and play hockey. It got pretty tough. I studied on the buses when we were travelling and when we got home late some nights I might not go to school the next morning." The Hockey Study Committee found that in Ontario there was a significant difference between the achievements of students who played hockey for teams *not affiliated* with their school and those of other students. "After a similar start in Grade 9, a divergent pattern of school behavior began to appear which became most pronounced around the fourth and fifth years of secondary schooling . . . . In terms of completion of Grade 13, only 5.9 per cent of the 511 [junior "A"] hockey players graduated as compared with 10.7 percent of the non- [junior "A"] hockey-playing group." A similar study among 273 players in Saskatchewan found a 64.4 percent withdrawal rate. Bad grades and dropouts are the inevitable result of the NHL's insistence that juniors play a schedule — 62 season games, plus playoffs in the case of the OHA Major Junior "A" — only slightly less gruelling than the one the pros themselves play. There are other ways of developing hockey players, and not necessarily at the expense of their education. American colleges, for instance, play only 24 games a season plus playoffs, and yet Canadian players of the calibre of Ken Dryden, Tony Esposito, Keith Magnuson and Red Berenson have moved successfully through the U.S. college system into the NHL.

The NHL's attitude towards players reflects its attitude towards hockey. It has always been a taker. It has contributed very little, for instance, to the technical improvement of the game. Its preoccupation has been discovering talent, not developing it. NHL coaches like Punch Imlach are recruiters, not teachers. With few exceptions — Conn Smythe in the old days, Johnny Wilson today — they rely almost entirely on the maturing of natural talent. They find the future stars of the game when they are 14 and play them in as many games as possible, the players being expected to develop the technical skills on their own. The same is true of overall fitness. Shortly before the 1972-73 season, former all-star defenceman Carl Brewer, considering a comeback with the Toronto Maple Leafs, was asked how he would get into shape: "Oh, that's easy," he replied. "You don't have to be in top shape to play in that league. I'll just run a few miles every day and play some shinny up at a rink where you can play all day for $2. Those guys are almost as good as anybody you'd see in the NHL." After two rushes, most NHL players need a rest, and no wonder. The poverty of NHL coaching has never been more apparent than in the five years since expansion, when natural stars like Frank Mahovlich and Bobby Orr have become superstars because so few of the less gifted players have had the skills to compensate. If the coaching were there — as it is in American football or Russian hockey — players like Mahovlich and Orr would be up against players who make up for deficiencies in natural ability with a disciplined knowledge of the game's skills. In 1969, Anatoli Tarasov observed in a book Team Canada coach Harry Sinden began reading only after the recent Canada-Russia series began:

I have seen nothing new at the training sessions of the professional teams. I doubt if I have purposely not been shown what is new. What I saw recently was the same thing I saw when we first toured Canada in 1957. Everything was practically identical. The content of the training process is essentially unchanged. Perhaps there is no real need for changes in the training process for games by the teams of the Canadian-American league. The teams have played an accustomed brand of hockey for many years, a brand that satisfies the clubs and the spectators and, therefore, the trainers have no intention of changing or modernizing their methods. What is new is to be found only within the possibilities of search of each separate player.

Think how good the Orrs, Mahovliches, Hulls and Espositos would be if they enjoyed systematic coaching from the likes of Tarasov and Vsevolod Bobrov. Think how good Wayne Cashman and Bill Goldsworthy would be if someone taught them to play the game instead of fight. Lloyd Percival has been telling us that for years, but hardly anybody listened.

The major problem is that Canadians now learn the game under NHL rules. Kids who play hockey in which there is unlimited bodychecking — as there is in NHL — seldom learn to skate properly because they are too busy looking out for a check. "A boy can always learn to keep his chin up when he's 15," says Bill L'Heureux, professor of physical education at the University of Western Ontario, "but by then it's usually too late to learn to skate, and skating is 80 per cent of the game. We should let the younger boys learn under international rules if we want them really to play hockey — but we can't because the NHL sets the rules." Tarasov once dumbfounded a group of Canadian sportswriters by asking them who was the top Canadian hockey strategist. They could not answer because they did not know. We do not debate hockey strategy. We have no leaders in the scientific development of the game. So kids learn what they see on television — dumping-in-the-puck and clutch-and-grab — and their parents can only shout at the referee.

The NHL has been similarly bankrupt in the area of safety. Although it has a tremendous investment in the health of its players, it has behaved as if anything to minimize the chance of injury would be an act of cowardice. In 1950, Clarence Campbell pooh-poohed hockey helmets as "too undignified," and that view has persisted, despite recurring head injuries (like the one Ted Green sustained in a fight with Wayne Maki in 1970, and the one that caused the death of Bill Masterson of Minneapolis in 1968). In 1970, the NHL voted a paltry $5,000 for helmet research. Jacques Plante had to threaten a sit-down strike in 1959 before the Montreal Canadiens allowed him to wear a facemask, and yet the mask has undoubtedly lengthened the careers of many NHL goalies. Fortunately, amateur hockey has in this one instance ignored the NHL's example. In 1971, the CAHA made helmets compulsory.

There is another sense in which the NHL has been a taker, and of all the wrongs it has committed against Canadian hockey, it is by far the worst. In its preoccupation with recruiting the best of the country's young players, and through its control of Canadian amateur hockey, the NHL has helped create an environment in which hockey is played only by youngsters and only as long as there is the possibility they might make the NHL. It is no accident that the number of boys playing hockey in Canada drops off dramatically after the age of 15, the age when scouts believe they can tell whether a boy has any chance of making hockey a career. Under the old sponsorship system, an amateur club might ice a number of peewee, bantam and midget teams but rarely more than one juvenile or junior team, thus making it impossible for any boy who could not make the team after his sixteenth birthday to remain in organized hockey. In 1969, the Task Force on Sport for Canadians found that in Québec there were 50,000 registered players between the ages of 9 and 15 but only 100 boys playing junior hockey. In 1971, the CAHA registered 84,000 bantams and 58,000 midgets but only 21,800 juveniles, 10,000 juniors and 1,706 junior "A" players. What happened to the boys who got left out along the way? They may not be good enough ever to play the game professionally, but does that mean they should not have been given the opportunity to play the game at all? The problem is a shortage of facilities. Nowhere in Canada has the construction of rinks kept pace with the growth in the teenage population. Ice time is scarce and, the purpose of amateur hockey being to develop players for the NHL, what little there is of it is hoarded for the boys with the most talent. The house league teams get maybe half an hour of hockey a week. The all-star teams get five. So the boy who develops at age 11 has a much better chance of becoming a good player than the boy who might develop at 15: he gets almost 10 times as much ice time. By the time the late-developer matures, he is several seasons behind. As for the majority of boys who never develop to professional standards but who enjoy the game just the same, the only time they might get ice time is at four o'clock on a Sunday morning or some equally unmanageable hour and, in most cases, they just give the game up.

They give it up for other reasons, too. The spirit of the age, if not always the practice, is peace, hedonism and individualism, and the example of hockey, the cheap unsportsmanlike play in the NHL, the frenzied compulsion to win in the little leagues, is alien to these values. The kids play the game for a few years as a ritual, and then happily quit. As a result, not very many Canadians play the game we call our national sport. Despite the soaring teenage registrations of the CAHA, there are just two kinds of hockey in this country: the hockey we play for a few brief years during adolescence, and the hockey a few hundred professionals provide as a television spectacle. Left out are hundreds of thousands of Canadians who ski and curl, play golf and tennis, who love hockey as much as they did when they were kids but who have been relegated to the sidelines as spectators. We play hockey to win, we play hockey to make money, but we have forgotten what it is to play hockey for fun. That, more than anything else, signals the death of the game.

Killing the
National Team

Andy Mann laid down his paper, removed his glasses, and relaxed in the big chair, exclaiming to his sixteen-year-old son, "Well! Joe, that's just too bad. Somebody should do something about it."

"About what, Dad?" enquired junior.

"It says here," his dad explained as he pointed to a sports editorial, "that Canada will never win another Olympic hockey title.

"Yes, Joe," concluded Andy, "Canada just can't afford to let the world think our young men are losing their vigor and courage. Our national esteem is certain to suffer, and somebody in this country should do something about it."

"Why don't you be that somebody, Dad?" ventured the lad. "You keep telling me that anything worthwhile is worth fighting for. Why don't you gather a team of good boys around sixteen or seventeen years old? Get them to promise to stay amateur for four years; then train them specially for the next Winter Olympics?"

—from Foster Hewitt's novel,
Hello, Canada, and Hockey Fans in the United States, *1950*

Twelve years after the fictitious Andy Mann led the Gloster Greys to the Olympic hockey championship, a real-life Canadian convinced the Canadian Amateur Hockey Association that he, too, could regain the world hockey crown for Canada with a team selected from the country's best junior amateur players. His name was Father David Bauer, and for eight years he and his many supporters struggled to find the best young players, give them good jobs or schooling, keep them together, and mould them into a team that would bring back the world championship, last won for Canada by the Trail Smoke-Eaters in 1961. But unlike the Gloster Greys, Father Bauer's national team never succeeded. The National Hockey League saw to that. And, saw to it, too, that it became the sole beneficiary of the years of work and at least $500,000 in public funds that had gone into the making of the National Team.

It was not always necessary for Canada to field a special team to seek the world hockey championship. In the early years, whichever team won the Canadian senior amateur championship Allan Cup was unbeatable overseas. The Winnipeg Falcons became European celebrities overnight when they breezed through the first international hockey championship, held as part of the Antwerp Olympic Games in 1920. In the first official Winter Olympics, held four years later in Chamonix, France, the Toronto Granites beat seven opponents by a total score of 149–3, despite soft ice and the absence of boards, which were not adopted by international rules until 1932. In the 1928 Winter Olympics at St. Moritz, the University of Toronto Grads were so powerful they were granted a bye into the final round. There, they demolished Sweden, Switzerland and Great Britain by scores of 11–0, 13–0 and 14–0 respectively. Canada's lop-sided victories became an annual affair in 1930, when the International Ice

Hockey Federation began staging world championships in non-Olympic years. In 1937, the Kimberley Dynamiters won their nine games by a total score of 64–0.

Canada's domination of these early series was only natural. In those days the English won the soccer games, the Finns the distance races. Although Europeans had played hockey or something like it for centuries, Canadians refined the game, perfected its skills and invented its equipment. (In the 1938 world tournament in Prague, 181 of the 185 players wore Canadian-made skates, and 166 used Canadian-made sticks.) Hockey was our specialty. Before the outbreak of the Second World War, we suffered only two losses in international play, one to the United States in 1933 and one to Great Britain in 1936. (The latter was a questionable defeat. The Port Arthur Bear Cats, standing in that year for the defending Allan Cup champion Halifax Wolverines, easily qualified for the final round despite a 2–1 loss to Great Britain in the qualifying round. But the organizers of the series decided to count the result of the preliminary game as a final round score, and no final round game was arranged between the two teams. The manager of the British team was an Irishman, J. F. "Bunny" Ahearne, who later became president of the IIHF.) Canadian supremacy in world hockey continued after the war, despite growing competition from Czechoslovakia, which upset the Sudbury Wolves in Stockholm in 1949. The Royal Canadian Air Force Flyers, sent overseas when the CAHA decided the Montreal Royals could not meet Avery Brundage's strict amateur standards, captured the 1948 Olympic championship in St. Moritz, and in Oslo in 1952 the Edmonton Mercurys did the same. But that 1952 gold medal was to mark the end of Canada's Golden Age in international hockey.

Nineteen-fifty-two was the first year the Soviet Union participated in the Olympics. After the Bolshevik Revolution, the International Olympic Committee, ignoring its own precept that "sport and politics do not mix," excluded representatives of the new workers' republic. After the Second World War, when the Soviets were briefly considered allies, the IOC invited them to participate in the 1948 Games. They declined, still recovering from war and too busy for sport. But by the 1952 Summer Olympics in Helsinki, they were ready to demonstrate the ambition and the scientific approach to training and competition that have since led them to breakthrough performances in virtually every sport: at Helsinki they carried off 68 medals and led in the unofficial team standing until the final day of competition. Nineteen-fifty-four was the first year the Soviets entered the world hockey championships. In the final game against the East York Lyndhursts, a strengthened Senior "B" club sent as Canadian representatives when no Senior "A" club was interested, the Russians skated effortlessly to a 7–2 victory and became world champions.

The Canadian public was shocked. Editorial writers bewailed our lost pride. Conn Smythe offered to take the Maple Leafs to Europe "immediately" to avenge Canada's fallen reputation. Remember, this was in the depths of the Cold War, when the Soviet Union was seen as a nation of rapists and murderers, and even in Canada echoes of McCarthyism forced critical journalists, professors and filmmakers to step carefully. In response to the public outcry, the CAHA insisted that the Allan Cup winner should represent Canada in all future world tournaments. Communities began strengthening their Senior "A" teams as if preparing for the religious wars. For a few years it worked. In 1955, bolstered by reinstated professionals, the Penticton Vees regained the world championship by blanking Russia 5–0 in the final game. In 1958 — Canada did not send a team in 1957 — the Whitby Dunlops (Harry Sinden was the captain) won the title again. In 1959, it was the Belleville McFarlands. But nothing had really changed. While the Russians, the Swedes, the English, the Germans, the Italians were building new facilities and experimenting with new techniques, Canadians indulged themselves in post-war affluence. In 1954, the federal government abolished the 11-year-old National Physical Fitness Act, public interest having waned and the civil servants responsible for it having become too vociferous in their demands for better programmes. Nowhere was our cavalier attitude towards sport better illustrated than in the Olympics, where the approach that brought us medals in Paris (1924), Amsterdam (1928), Los Angeles (1932) and Berlin (1936) left us sucking air in London (1948), Helsinki (1952), Melbourne (1956) and Rome (1960). It was the same with hockey. After 1954, even the most carefully selected Canadian team of salaried "amateurs" could place no better than second in the Olympics. In 1956, the Kitchener-Waterloo Dutchmen finished third behind the USSR and the United States. In 1960, they finished second to the United States.

The Trail Smoke-Eaters won what was to be Canada's last world championship in 1961. But it was clear by then that the Allan Cup winner could no longer be expected to skate circles around the rest of the world. The burden on the communities supporting senior hockey was too great. Accelerating urbanization made it more difficult for towns like Whitby, Trail, Belleville and Kitchener to keep young men from leaving for the jobs and big lights of cities like Montreal and Toronto. If a boy was a promising hockey player, the NHL would simply buy him away. The costs of maintaining a senior team were becoming prohibitive. Teams bargained for top "amateurs" and used-up pros, and then struggled to maintain them at the standard to which they had been accustomed. Belleville's 1959 World Amateur Champions had been paid $263,833 in salaries during the previous three years, a fact revealed by a judicial inquiry into the disappearance of $110,000 in city funds. The money had been paid to the hockey team, a common practice in many Senior "A" communities, although usually it was out in the open. By 1962, the Vees, the Dunlops, the McFarlands and the Dutchmen had folded for lack of money. In 1962, the Galt Terriers, a share-the-wealth club which included former NHLer Tod Sloan, had to pass the hat at exhibition games to raise the $15,000 it needed to compete in the world tournament in Colorado Springs. Despite the absence of the Russians, who stayed home to rebuild, the Terriers could place no higher than second behind the Swedes.

Public breastbeating continued. When the Kitchener-Waterloo Dutchmen lost to the United States in 1960, Kingston Alderman George Webb sent the team a telegram: "From the birthplace of hockey, I'm going to call for an official day of mourning and ask that our flag be lowered to half-mast. Congratulations for nothing." But others reacted more positively. In 1962, Frank Boucher, a veteran of 29 seasons as player and coach with the New York Rangers, and at the time commissioner of the Saskatchewan Junior Hockey League, suggested that Canada be represented by an all-star team of graduated juniors. (IIHF rules precluded obvious professionals.) Boucher's team would be financed by exhibition games all across Canada, the players remaining amateur, receiving only expenses. Boucher's all-star concept was shared by Jack Roxborough, then president of the CAHA, although he made a slightly different proposal. Arguing that it would not be feasible to assemble a junior team because the NHL controlled the best juniors, he suggested the creation of an all-star senior team which would be held together for more than one season. It would play in world tournaments and the Olympic competitions from which reinstated pros were banned.

But it was Father David Bauer who came up with the plan the CAHA adopted in the summer of 1962. Father Bauer's idea was to collect the best graduating juniors and Canadian college players in Canada and the United States, and assemble them at a university where they could play hockey and continue their education. Father Bauer had four objectives for his National Team:

1. *To establish an organization that would enable Canada to compete effectively in international competition with the increasingly skilful teams of other countries.*

2. *To create a new ideal for Canadian youth by associating excellence in hockey with excellent opportunities for personal education and technical development.*

3. *To help increase awareness of the significance of amateur hockey and to give support thereby to the CAHA in arranging an agreement with professional hockey that would guarantee to the amateur body true independence of operation.*

4. *To provide a focus for Canadian unity on the level of athletics that could bring together, for a truly national effort, all parts of this country.*

Father Bauer proposed that his team begin practices in the summer of 1963 and first represent Canada at the 1964 Olympic Games in Innsbruck, Austria. The CAHA's acceptance of his plan came just in time. The following winter, in Stockholm, the Trail Smoke-Eaters, the last Allan Cup champions to represent Canada overseas, placed fourth in the world tournament, Canada's worst showing since the Winnipeg Falcons' victory in Antwerp in 1920.

The marriage of hockey and education was important to Father Bauer. A former Memorial Cup player himself, he had turned down an offer to turn professional with the Boston Bruins in 1946, "because when the world is in turmoil, the mind wants to know why. That's basically what happened to me. I wanted to get an education, not as an alternative means of getting the financial benefits I could get as a pro hockey player, but because it was important for me to see what one could learn about truth." He accepted religious vows and became a priest. Ever since Father Henry Carr led St. Michael's College to the Allan Cup in 1910, there has been a powerful sporting tradition among Canadian Basilians, the order to which Father Bauer belongs. So it was inevitable he would coach hockey and bring to it his conviction that it should be part of a broader education. In the late 1950s, when Conn Smythe was telling national television audiences that too much schooling ruined hockey players (because it gave them what Smythe derided as a "jellyfish handshake"), coach Bauer of the St. Michael's College Majors conducted fewer practices and carried six extra players so that every player had as much time as possible for his books. No St. Michael's player was required to dress for all 54 games of the regular OHA Junior "A" schedule. In 1961 St. Michael's won the Memorial Cup.

Father Bauer's experiment with the National Team began on a windy, chilly day in August, 1963, when 33 players he had personally scouted assembled for tryouts at the University of Alberta in Edmonton. It was a shoestring operation from the beginning. Unable to find plane fare, 25 players drove west from Toronto in a new bus that defenceman

Barry McKenzie had arranged to deliver to a customer in Calgary. Few comforts were added when that autumn the team moved to the University of British Columbia in Vancouver. The team's 22 members were boarded in a small house and adjacent pre-fab cottage, sharing just one bathroom. Extra exhibition games — as many as five a week — were fitted in to pay the bills. The austerity of that first winter gave the team a sense of togetherness and sportsmanship that was never altogether dissipated in its seven years of competition.

Despite an indifferent exhibition record, by the time the Olympics opened in Innsbruck in February, 1964, Father Bauer's Nats were playing at their peak: seven games in ten days. Led by Seth Martin, Rod Seiling and Brian Conacher, the team outplayed the Swedes 3–1, came from behind to beat the United States 8-6 and easily defeated Germany, Switzerland and Finland. The last two games against Czechoslovakia and Russia were cliff-hangers. Canada led Czechoslovakia 1–0 until the 11-minute mark of the final period when goalie Seth Martin was injured in a collision. With four minutes remaining, and Ken Broderick in the nets, the Czechs scored three unanswered goals. It was the same story hours later against the unbeaten Russians. After two periods the teams were tied 2–2, but the Russians scored in the early minutes of the final period and the Canadians were unable to reply. The team's record of five wins and two losses was the same as Czechoslovakia's and Sweden's, but on the basis of goals for and against it placed fourth. Not quite the beginning Canadians had hoped for, but a victory for the National Team concept, nevertheless. The Nats had demonstrated to Canada what the rest of the world had known for some time; namely that competitive athletics and scholarship are compatible. If Bauer could get the right players, such a team *could* bring back the world champion-ship. The 1964 team had successfully demonstrated that Canadians could play by the rules. There was always a sour aftertaste to the victories of stick-swinging teams like the Vees and the McFarlands. Bauer's team presented a different image. "This is the cleanest and best-mannered hockey team to come to Europe in the past 30 years," commented a senior Swiss hockey official. The difference did not go unnoticed back home. Many Canadian newspapers ran editorials echo-ing sentiments like this: "The sportsmanship of Canada's young Olympic hockey players adds up to a moral victory that is as good as a gold medal . . ."

It was a beginning full of promise, but somehow the Nationals never lived up to it. Except for their dramatic vic-tory in the 1967 Centennial Tournament in Winnipeg (the team had moved to Winnipeg in the fall of 1964), they were unable to beat the Russians. Nor did they regain the world championship. In the 1965 world championships in Tampere, Finland, the Czechs bombed the out-of-shape Nats 8–0 in the fifth game, after which they never won another, finishing fourth. In 1966, in Ljubljana, the team was the victim of refereeing so poor that even the captain of the Czech team called it unfair. In 1967, in Vienna, the Nats finished third, although tied in points with second-place Sweden. At the 1968 Olympics in Grenoble, they placed third. In the 1969 world championships in Stockholm they placed fourth, with a record of four wins and six losses, their worst showing ever. In seven years, Father Bauer's Nationals played 286 games, winning 184 of them, losing 76 and tying 26. But against the Russians, they won only 6 of 33 games (2 ties), and against the Czechs 14 of 34 (4 ties). They won 4 of 10 exhibition games against NHL clubs. The team's best record was in the classroom: 31 of 82 players received university degrees and 42 others, many of whom played for the team only a year, earned degree credits.

The problem had been getting players. More precisely, the problem had been the National Hockey League, whose governors saw the National Team as a threat to their monopoly on Canadian players. Every player on the team was on an NHL protected list. Among the 40 players invited to the Nats' first training camp in 1963 were 10 professional prospects of the Toronto Maple Leafs. In 1966, Bobby Orr rejected the Boston Bruins' first contract offer and threatened to play for the Nationals if they did not meet his terms. Serge Savard was ready to tell the Canadiens the same thing. With players like Orr and Savard, the Nats would challenge the NHL's prestige and create a serious player drought. And with expansion imminent, the NHL would soon need double the number of players. Its course was clear: destroy the National Team.

That is exactly what happened. The NHL prevented Father Bauer and Jackie McLeod, who became the Nationals' coach in 1966, from getting players. In 1964, the Nats needed some extra scoring power. Father Bauer asked Sam Pollack, the Canadiens' general manager, for a three-week loan of Yvan Cournoyer of the Montreal Junior Canadiens. Pollack refused. Later that year, Cournoyer was loaned to the Canadiens for five NHL games, making him officially a professional and thus eliminating any chance he would ever play for the Nats. (Pollack had always been touchy about Olympic teams. In 1959, Kitchener-Waterloo manager Ernie Goman approached Wayne Carleton, then playing for the Peterborough Petes, a Canadiens' farm team, about joining the Dutchmen for the Squaw Valley Olympic Games. Pollack called the CAHA and demanded Goman's suspension for "tampering".) The NHL tried to buy away those players the Nats actually succeeded in signing. In 1967, a few days before the Centennial Tournament in Winnipeg, the Minnesota North Stars offered Gary Dineen $75,000 to quit the National Team. Only after some agonizing did he decline, deciding to abide by his commitment to remain with the Nats until the 1968 Olympics. "The pros still considered us their property," says Brian Conacher, a three-year veteran with the Nationals who later signed a $35,000 contract with the Leafs. "Every player on the team always received an invitation to training camp. They wanted us."

The NHL used its control over the definition of "amateur" to prevent the team from reinstating retired pros in non-Olympic years. Carl Brewer had to threaten court action against the Toronto Maple Leafs in 1966 before they would permit him to play for the Nats. The Leafs — not the CAHA — owned the power to reinstate him as an "amateur". As part of its 1967 agreement with the NHL, the CAHA ruled that none of its teams (including the National Team) could "approach, negotiate or discuss employment with any unsigned drafted player before October 21 in any playing year without the prior consent [of the NHL]". The NHL draft has no legal status. An "unsigned drafted player" is still an amateur. The effect of this agreement was to force the National Team to take second place to the NHL in the competition for junior amateurs, and a distant second place at that: the Nationals were prohibited from discussing hockey with players graduating from junior ranks until two full months after they began practising. In another clause of the 1967 agreement, the CAHA undertook not to spend any of its player development funds on the National Team. The CAHA gets the money for the players the NHL drafts from the ranks of Canadian juniors. In a letter to Health Minister

John Munro, acting CAHA president Earl Dawson attempted to justify the betrayal as follows:

There's nothing wrong with this, is there? Because the monies they pay us are used to develop hockey players. Once the boy makes the National Team, he is a hockey player, otherwise he wouldn't be on the National Team. And they're giving us half a million dollars a year which we pour into the training and developing of hockey players. Many of these boys for whom the professional people have given us money to develop, end up on the National Team. They [the NHL] are saying that they are not prepared to directly subsidize a team which is in fact in competition with them — and we in the CAHA see nothing wrong with that.

There was one final restriction. On September 29, 1968, the CAHA national executive voted unanimously that "Canada's National Team not recruit junior-age players," a ruling that denied the team access to almost 12,000 registered junior hockey players. Having imposed the same restriction on the NHL the year before, the CAHA was making certain the National Team did not enjoy any advantages. The CAHA made it impossible for the National Team to function.

According to a paper called *The Unmaking of our Canadian National Hockey Team,* by Terry O'Malley, a seven-year veteran with the Nats, it was the rising costs of maintaining the team, combined with the frustrations of losing, that finally forced a change. With the advent of a second team based in Ottawa, annual costs soared to $200,000, which was more than the CAHA could afford. In 1967, a group of prominent Canadians, led by former Ontario Liberal Leader John Wintermeyer, CPR President Ian Sinclair and the late Max Bell, created the Canadian Hockey Foundation to raise funds for the National Team and to provide scholarships at Canadian universities. A few months later, the Task Force on Sport for Canadians, headed by Toronto businessman Harold Rea, skier Nancy Greene and Québec physician Paul Desruisseaux, recommended that the federal government create a special corporation to finance *and manage* the National Team. Hockey Canada, as the corporation was to be called, would be composed of representatives from the NHL, the CAHA, the universities, the government and the public. The Task Force argued that only a widely representative Hockey Canada could smooth over relations between the National Team and the NHL. The federal government agreed. When Hockey Canada was finally incorporated in 1969, its first board of directors included Wintermeyer, Sinclair and Bell (the Canadian Hockey Foundation had been dissolved) as well as Father Bauer, Earl Dawson, Alan Eagleson, Douglas Fisher, Charles Hay, W. J. Hopwood, Gordon Juckes, Lou Lefaive, David Molson, Maurice Regimbal and the late Stafford Smythe. Bell was elected chairman, and Hay, the retired president of Gulf Oil, president.

One of Hockey Canada's first acts was the appointment of L. A. "Hap" Emms, a former general manager of the Boston Bruins, as general director of the National Team. Emms had watched the Nats flounder through the 1969 world tournament in Stockholm, and sent back this report:

It is apparent to me that it was necessary for them to beg, borrow or steal players . . . to ice a hockey team for international ice hockey competition, regardless of calibre. Under these circumstances, I feel they did the best job possible, and are to be commended for their efforts, but obviously this is not good enough for international competition if we are to be represented as we would like Canada to be. Under the existing agreements with the National Hockey League and the CAHA it is, in my opinion, an impossibility to organize and operate a competitive national team to represent Canada in international competition.

Emms' job was to strengthen the Nationals for the 1970 world tournament. In one of his first reports to Hockey Canada in April, 1969, he complained that almost all the players he wanted to keep from the 1969 team were being offered contracts by the NHL. He went on to outline what he believed were the minimum requirements for the successful operation of the National Team:

1. *Increase the junior age limit to 21 years and the pro-amateur draft to 20 years. This would benefit Hockey Canada in the development of players. American college scouts are taking advantage of this present age limit, education-wise, in luring Canadian players to their colleges.*
2. *Abolish the pro-amateur draft for 1969, or Hockey Canada be allowed to protect 10 players from this draft.*
3. *Should the junior age limit or the pro-amateur draft remain as at present, or change, Hockey Canada should have the privilege of protecting 10 players in 1969, 5 players in 1970, and 5 players in 1972. This would be repetitive in succeeding years. Drafting price of the players from the National Team to professional clubs would have to be agreed upon by both parties.*

But despite its representation on Hockey Canada's board of directors and its public statements of support (Smythe had promised to loan the team three Maple Leafs), the NHL refused to cooperate. At a committee meeting in Ottawa on May 8, 1969, with Lou Lefaive, Douglas Fisher, Emms and John Munro, Clarence Campbell and David Molson delivered an ultimatum. According to the minutes, they "disapproved" of the team-in-being concept. They said the NHL could not "make any arrangements" to provide the National Team with draft rights to Junior "A" players. They said they were "not optimistic, from the point of view of quality, that many worthwhile players could be freed for the National Team by reinstatement of professionals". They made it clear that Smythe could not "deliver" three Maple Leafs to the National Team because "it would not be acceptable" to the other NHL owners. Campbell and Molson proposed an alternative to the team-in-being concept; an "ad hoc team" assembled in the weeks prior to an international tournament with players the NHL would supply. It was an impossible choice. The NHL was telling Hockey Canada it was not prepared to support a Bauer-style team. The NHL was telling Hockey Canada that unless the National Team was dismantled, it would continue to prevent the team from getting the country's best young players. Either you play our game, it was saying, or no game at all. Hockey Canada accepted. All but Emms. He quit.

Several weeks later, in July of 1969, Hockey Canada petitioned the IIHF for an open tournament in which NHL players would be eligible. In reply, the IIHF tentatively approved two eligibility changes for the 1970 World Tournament in Montreal and Winnipeg. The first would permit nine non-NHL professional players per team. The second would permit governing bodies like the CAHA to reinstate professional players as "amateurs" anytime up to February 10, 1970, two days before the tournament was to open. But

Avery Brundage, the octogenarian president of the International Olympic Committee, rumbled that players who competed in such a professionalized tournament might be ruled ineligible for the 1972 Winter Olympics. The IIHF retreated. At an emergency meeting in Geneva on January 4, 1970, it reversed its ruling on the eligibility of non-NHL professionals. But it left the instant reinstatement clause perfectly intact, so nothing had really changed: Canada could still declare any professional player an amateur up until two days before the tournament was to begin. But Hockey Canada stormed out of Europe, cancelled the 1970 tournament and withdrew the Canadian team. (For the next two years it would forbid *any* team — even a team of Toronto eight-year-olds called the Hunts Tomatoes — to play in international competition.) Explaining the decision back in Canada, Charles Hay took a low blow at the players Hockey Canada had already assembled for the tournament. "Canada has 635 professional hockey players," he said. "That's about 30 teams. So what we send over is number 31. Other countries send over their best." Except in Winnipeg, where the cancellation of the tournament meant the loss of $500,000 in anticipated revenue ($300,000 in advance ticket sales had to be returned), the press parroted the Hockey Canada line: If we could not send our best, we should not send anyone at all. Within weeks the National Team was disbanded.

It was — and still is — popularly held that Canada could never regain the world hockey championship with a team of amateurs. Yet this proposition was never really tested. Father Bauer wanted to train a team specifically for the world championship, the way all other hockey-playing countries do. The NHL permitted him neither the players nor the funds to give it a try. There was nothing special about the amateur status of the Canadian team. By CAHA definition, the players were amateur only because they were not considered professional by the NHL. In terms of the Olympic code, they were as professional as any Russian. Most of the players on the National Team were on some sort of athletic scholarship — then outlawed by Olympic eligibility rules — and several were receiving salaries. Goaltender Ken Dryden had turned down a $75,000 offer from the Montreal Canadiens to sign with the National Team at $10,000 a year.

The beneficiary of Canada's withdrawal from international hockey was the NHL. Among the members of what Charles Hay called our thirty-first team were Ken Dryden, Danny O'Shea, Gerry Pinder, Billy Macmillan, Denis Dupere, Brian Glennie and Ab Demarco, all of whom later went to the NHL. The loser, of course, was Canadian hockey. With the National Team gone, the NHL was free to continue skimming off the cream of Canada's young hockey players and sending them off to the United States to make money for the likes of Weston Adams. In a sense it hurt all Canadian sport. Canada had been the National Team's point of reference. If it had survived, it might have encouraged other Canadian sportsmen, who all too frequently look to the United States for leadership, to find Canadian solutions to Canadian problems. The death of the National Team was also the death of an idea: the marriage of sport and career. It is difficult to identify with the NHL player who devotes his life to hockey and nothing else. The members of the National Team taught school and studied law and played hockey as well. They could have shown us that sport can be a part of a normal life and responsibilities. So bang the drum slowly. The National Team was a noble experiment that got it in the neck.

There is more to the story. In the spring of 1972, the Soviets agreed with the CAHA to play an eight-game exhibition series against a team of Canadian professionals assembled by Hockey Canada. Having scuttled the National Team at the urging of the NHL, it was only natural that Hockey Canada would turn over to the NHL the selection of the Canadian team. And that is exactly what Hockey Canada did. As a result, Canadian players like Bobby Hull, Gerry Cheevers, Derek Sanderson and J. C. Tremblay, who had jumped from the NHL to the new World Hockey Association, were excluded. Team Canada meant Team NHL. The decision to limit Team Canada to only those players who had signed NHL contracts was made by Hockey Canada's board of directors on August 2. The vote was 9 to 2. Voting in favour were the federal government's two representatives, Lou Lefaive and Sam Weston; the NHL's two representatives, Clarence Campbell and Harold Ballard; the CAHA's three representatives, Earl Dawson, Joseph Kryczka and Gordon Juckes; the NHL players' representative, Alan Eagleson; and the provincial government's representative, William Clark. Voting against were Father Bauer and John Wintermeyer. After it was all over, Alan Eagleson defended the sellout this way. "Here in Canada," he told reporters, "we can put country before players, but we must remember that the majority of [coach Harry] Sinden's choices are employed in the United States and we cannot expect the American owners to put Canada first. It is unrealistic." John Wintermeyer's response was more heart-felt. "Once again," he said, "idealism has been subordinated to economics."

Despite Prime Minister Trudeau's well-publicized plea to Clarence Campbell to allow Bobby Hull to play in the Canada-Russia series (notice, he petitioned Campbell, not

Hockey Canada), the federal government did nothing to intervene. The Liberals have always played ball with the multi-national corporations, and the NHL is no exception. In the fall of 1969, for instance, two Toronto sports writers suggested that Hockey Canada recruit Bobby Hull, then in the midst of a public contract dispute with the Chicago Black Hawks. It was John Munro, the federal minister who pays Hockey Canada's bills, who stepped in and killed the idea. "Now remember," he said, "Hockey Canada is representative. Mr. Hull has a contract with the NHL. Hockey Canada cannot encourage him to breach that contract unless it wants a war — financial or otherwise — and no cooperation from the NHL. We know how a lack of cooperation in recent years hurt the National Team."

The Canada-Russia series took place between September 2 and September 28. After a shocking 7-3 loss in the opening game in Montreal, the Canadian team grew stronger game by game, and by the last one in Moscow had drawn level with the Russians. It was a peculiar position for the NHL all-stars: regarded as overwhelming favourites, even by the Russians, they had fallen behind and were now, in the last period of the last game, underdogs, gamely fighting back. With a minute left, the score was tied 5-5.

No matter what the outcome, everyone at that point agreed that the series had produced the best hockey anyone had seen anywhere in years — the best Canadian hockey since the Montreal Canadiens were playing at their peak in the late 1950s. In Moscow, the belligerent, slow-skating NHL selects became a new team — spirited, diligent, skating both ways, and scoring, too. Canadians were rediscovering the game. The team itself seemed to feed on the revelation that they were better players than the NHL had ever allowed them to be and started playing with a style and mastery that showed they could, if they wanted to, beat the Russians. Out of one international series came proof that if we cared enough, this better game of hockey could go on and on, down to the smallest league in the most remote town in Canada. Canadian hockey was being remade in Moscow.

But if the series was demonstrating the strength of Canadian hockey, it was also revealing some weaknesses. No one, not even the Canadian players, disputed the Russians' superior conditioning. These were superbly trained athletes who could play with as much stamina in the third period as the first. Harry Sinden admitted that the Soviet team would have had an edge in conditioning even if the series had been played in the middle of the NHL regular season. But there was more to the Russian game than physical endurance. Their skating, passing, stickhandling and shooting were evidence of superior coaching techniques and a concept of the game that emphasizes finesse over rough play. Occasionally, they kicked and speared when the referees were not looking, but by comparison with some of the Canadian players they looked like gentlemen. The Canadians played with chips on their shoulders, threatening to brawl at the slightest provocation. During the seventh game Phil Esposito taunted the Russians with fists and throat-cutting gestures from the penalty box. In the first period of the final game Jean Paul Parise swung his stick menacingly at a referee. Someone on the Canadian bench threw a chair on the ice, and someone else hit the referee with a towel. Later on, Alan Eagleson scuffled with Soviet police and walked across the ice waving his fist at the Russian fans. Off the ice, the attitude of some of the Canadian players left something to be desired. Vic Hadfield, Richard Martin, Jocelyn Guevremont and Gilbert Perreault abandoned the team in Moscow when coach Sinden told them they would probably sit out the rest of the series. And a few days later Yvan Cournoyer suggested that the Canadian team might play better if the players were being paid. "If we do it again [play a series with the Russians]," said Eagleson, "I would want the players to be paid. It would be $5,000 for each player invited to a six-week training camp, $5,000 for making the team, and additional money for each game played."

But it would have been wrong to place all the blame for this on the players. They were the stars of the NHL. If their attitude detracted from the pride we took in their thrilling comeback in Moscow, well, that is the way the NHL had taught them to play the game. "If I held a goalie down in the NHL I would be cheered for it," explained Frank Mahovlich after he held Vladislav Tretiak out of the Soviet net for almost 15 seconds in the fourth game in Vancouver. If the Canadians were out of shape for most of the series, while the Russans seemed barely to be sweating, well, NHL coaching and conditioning has not changed significantly in 40 years. Nor was professional hockey likely to learn much from the series. Bobby Hull, the player coach of the Winnipeg Jets, was apologetic about it: "We can't expect our players to get in that kind of shape," he said. "It's our system." Phil Esposito was defiant: "I'm not interested in what style they play, what style we play. The idea is to score and prevent the other guys from scoring, no matter what style you play. I don't think our game will change at all." Even if the pros were willing to learn, what good would it do? Towards the end of the series, Gord Walker had written in *The Globe and Mail*: "Junior hockey [which feeds professional hockey] thrives on boisterous, brawling performance, and it's not going to change regardless of the Soviet lesson. Finesse is too hard to acquire. . . . If the Soviets think National Hockey League players are extremely crude and rough, they should view some of the Major Junior A games. Even NHL people have been astounded by the lack of discpline." And look at the response of those professional hockey people who *were* impressed by the European style of play: the American reaction to Sputnik in 1957 was to invest in a space programme to beat the Russians to the moon. The response of Harold Ballard, the president of the Toronto Maple Leafs, to the Russians' 7-3 victory in the opening game of the series, was to offer $1 million to Soviet star Valery Kharlamov.

Up until the last minute of that eighth game in Moscow, when the score was still tied 5-5, it would have been difficult to choose between the two teams. If the Russians had played a prettier style of hockey, the Canadians had demonstrated the individual brilliance that is the hallmark of the Canadian game, and the possibility seemed always to be lurking that at any moment they might explode and play the Soviets out of the rink. But at 19:26 of the third period, with just 34 seconds left in the game, Paul Henderson banged a rebound into the Soviet goal to give the Canadians a 6-5 victory and a one-game edge in the series. In the end, the stars of the NHL had not played better than the Russians, but they had shown more desire — which may have *little* to do with hockey but everything to do with winning.

The future of Team Canada? Hockey Canada chairman Douglas Fisher, who should know better, suggests that another time WHA players might be included on the team. But it was Harold Ballard who gave us a clearer look at the future. "This will be my last salvo," Ballard told *The Globe and Mail*. "I'm not going to have anything to do with future Russian series until they apply for an NHL franchise."

The Making of a
Hockey Empire

On November 22, 1917, the lone reporter in the Windsor Hotel dutifully waiting for news [from the annual meeting of the National Hockey Association] was Elmer Ferguson. . . . Out of the room came George Kennedy, smiling. The jovial Kennedy, owner of the Montreal Canadiens which he had purchased in 1910 for $7,500, took his friend Fergie by the arm and said, "Come on down to the bar, and I'll give you the full story."

In the bar Kennedy continued, and his excitement was visible. "We formed a new hockey league called the National Hockey League, and it's just like the National Hockey Association with one exception. We haven't invited Eddie Livingstone (owner of the Toronto team) to be part of the set-up."

Sam Lichtenhein, owner of the Montreal Wanderers, joined the pair, and hearing Kennedy's last remark, added: "Don't get us wrong, Elmer. We didn't throw Livingstone out; he's still got his franchise in the old National Hockey Association. He has his team, and we wish him well. The only problem is he's playing in a one-team league."

Tommy Gorman, of the Ottawa club, chortled over the maneuver. "Great day for hockey," he said. "Livingstone

was always arguing. Without him we can get down to the
business of making money."

— *Brian McFarlane,* 50 Years of Hockey, A History of the National
Hockey League, *1967.*

Tommy Gorman was not the first entrepreneur to equate
hockey with "the business of making money". Hockey has
been exploited for private profit almost from the moment,
sometime in the 1880s, it was first played on an enclosed
rink. But there have been *two* hockey traditions in Canada,
of which the commercial tradition is just one. The other is
the community tradition. At one time or another, in hundreds
of Canadian towns and cities, people chipped in to build
a rink and ice a hockey team, and many of these teams were
as good as any in the commercial leagues. But community
hockey died shortly after the Second World War, a casualty
of the National Hockey League. Once hockey became a
business it was inevitable that the men who owned it would
prey upon the community leagues, just as it was inevitable
that eventually they would seek the richer markets of the
United States. That is what "getting down to the business of
making money" has been all about.

Men have played games with curved sticks for centuries.
In the British Museum, there is a fragment of a Greek
sculpture (circa 478 BC) showing two men with curved
sticks facing one another in an alignment somewhat similar
to a present-day faceoff. In Amsterdam's Rijksmuseum, a
painting called Winter Landscape by the Dutch artist Henrick
Avercamp (1585-1634) shows boys playing a game on ice
that looks remarkably like the hockey we know today. So
hockey, or something like it, predates the period between
1783 and 1855 when it was first played in Canada by English
troops stationed in Halifax and Kingston. But here the game

was refined. A group of McGill students developed and publicized a set of rules in 1880, and hockey spread rapidly in Québec and eastern Ontario. The first organized league hockey was played on harbour ice in Kingston, a fact which persuaded the history committee of the Canadian Amateur Hockey Association to designate that city the "birthplace of hockey". The game did not arrive in Toronto until 1887 but became popular so quickly that within two years five sporting clubs were conducting regular matches. It was the same in the West. Three Winnipeg clubs were already in existence by 1890. The Manitoba Hockey Association was formed in 1892. Saskatchewan discovered the game three years later when, according to sports historian Henry Roxborough, a bundle of sticks was shipped to the wrong address. By 1904, the game had reached Dawson City in the Yukon, kindling such excitement that the following January gold miner Joe Boyle was persuaded to send the Dawson City Nuggets to Ottawa to challenge the Ottawa Silver Seven for the Stanley Cup. Hockey was the right game at the right place at the right time. The pace of Canadian life was quickening, with growing industrialization, urbanization and improved communications — in the census of 1901, 59.8 per cent of the Canadian labour force worked outside agriculture, and 37.5 per cent of the population lived in towns and cities — and hockey struck a responsive chord. Canadians were already curling, snowshoeing, skating and sleighing, but hockey was faster, more complex, more exciting to play and infinitely more interesting to watch.

It was an instant commercial success. In 1896, a box seat for a Stanley Cup game in Winnipeg between the Winnipeg Victorias and the Montreal Victorias (at the height of British Imperialism, the old queen was a favourite) cost $12, and this at a time when the average wage was 15 cents an hour and sirloin steak cost 10 cents a pound. In 1908, 7,000 tickets were sold for the playoff game in Montreal between the Wanderers and the Ottawa Senators, and many of them were resold by scalpers for as much as $125. These were playoff prices, but regular prices — $1.50, $1 and 50 cents — were still high enough to guarantee a comfortable profit. Gambling was widespread in Canada at the time. Whether or not there was proportionately more money wagered on sport then than now, the practice was certainly visible. Well-to-do sports fans staked what were large amounts of money even by today's standards on the popular sports of the day. When Toronto sculler Ned Hanlan raced Charles E. Courtney on the Potomac in 1880, something like $100,000 was wagered on the outcome. Hockey was no exception. Silver baron Noah Timmins bet $50,000 on a game between his Haileybury Seven and the Cobalt Silver Kings in 1910, and when Haileybury won 6-5 in overtime Timmins and other Haileybury supporters showered the ice with dollar bills.

Gambling played a part in turning hockey professional. Between the betting and the paying of admissions, a lot of money changed hands inside the arenas, and it was only a matter of time before hockey players would demand to be paid. The other spectator sports then popular, boxing, baseball and especially lacrosse, had been professional for a long time, so it was not as if hockey players were asking for something new. And although the belief in amateurism was strong among the military and members of the middle and upper classes who played hockey in the universities and private clubs, it meant little in the frontier mining towns, where working conditions were brutal and where there was no middle class to sustain it. It was in a mining town, Houghton, Michigan, near the giant Hecla copper mine, that the first professional hockey team was created in 1903 by a Canadian dentist named J. L. Gibson, who hired some players he had known in Kitchener for a team he called the Portage Lakes. Of course, players had been secretly paid well before 1903. The Kitchener team Dr. Gibson played for in 1898 had been expelled from the Ontario Hockey Association for professionalism, and the same year Ottawa goaltender Frank Chittick refused to dress for a playoff game because he had not been allotted his share of complimentary tickets — tickets he presumably would have sold. But the Portage Lakes brought professionalism out into the open and gave birth to the first professional hockey league, called the International Professional League. Although all the players were Canadian it included only one Canadian team: Sault Ste. Marie. Within a few years, professional leagues operated alongside amateur leagues in every part of Canada. In the Maritimes, there was the Maritime Pro League. In Ontario, the New Ontario League and the Ontario Pro League (dubbed the "trolley" league because the players travelled to and from games in Toronto, Kitchener, Brantford and Guelph on radial streetcars). On the Prairies, there were the Manitoba and Northwestern League and the Saskatchewan League, and, in British Columbia, the Boundary League. Even the amateur leagues began to relax their rules, and in 1907 the Eastern Canada Amateur Hockey Association decided to allow its teams to play pros, provided they declared who was paid (the lists were published in the newspapers). The first hockey salaries, according to Cyclone Taylor who played for the Portage Lakes, averaged $50 a week. Not bad, compared to the $12 to $15 a week you could earn if you were lucky enough to get a job working six 12-hour days in a factory or mine. The mining industry and professional hockey went hand in hand in the early days. In addition to Houghton and Sault Ste. Marie, Cobalt and

Haileybury, pro teams sprang up around the coal mines of Cape Breton, the gold mines of Kirkland Lake, the copper-zinc fields of Flin Flon, and the smelters of Trail. When the mining barons, their fortunes made, left the towns for the comforts of the big city, they took with them their interest in hockey. J. P. Bickell, a gold millionaire, was one of the owners of the Toronto St. Patricks and stayed on as a direc-tor when the team was sold to Conn Smythe and renamed the Toronto Maple Leafs. (The J. P. Bickell trophy is still awarded each year to the outstanding Leaf.)

Professional hockey was growing, but for many years after the turn of the century, in fact up until the Second World War, for every professional team in Canada there were 10 to 15 amateur teams representing private athletic clubs, universities, regiments and businesses. Many of them were far more popular than the professional clubs. The early pros were always being traded from team to team or jumping from league to league, while most of the amateur players grew up in the communities where they played their hockey. They worked in the banks or the mills, and people came to know them as neighbours and cheered twice as hard for them when they laced on their skates. The community teams were often as good as or better than the professional clubs. When six teams in the Eastern Canadian Amateur Hockey Associa-tion went professional in 1907, the Montreal Victorias, which remained amateur, still placed third in the standings. After the First World War, amateur teams were prohibited from playing professionals, which may have been just as well for the pros. "The Granites and the University of Toronto could beat the pros on their lunch hour," says Toronto sports columnist Ted Reeve. "They outdrew them, too."

But it is misleading to compare the "amateur" and "pro-fessional" traditions in Canadian hockey, because by 1920 many amateur teams had begun to pay their players — and not in the form of complimentary tickets, either. Between 1921 and 1924, Nels Stewart earned $100 a week playing amateur hockey in Cleveland. Other so-called amateurs were being similiarly remunerated. In 1921, Lester Patrick demanded a public investigation of the Alberta Big Four amateur league. The public and the government, he claimed, were being defrauded by the evasion of provincial amusement tax applicable to professional sport. In 1935, the Canadian Amateur Hockey Association decided to end the hypocrisy of under-the-table payments and permit players to sign legally binding contracts, to "capitalize on their ability as hockey players for the purpose of obtaining legitimate employment," and to accept compensation for time lost from work playing hockey. Two years later, the CAHA withdrew from the Amateur Athletic Union of Canada. So the words "amateur" and "professional" ceased to have much meaning. The distinction now was not between amateur and professional teams but community and commercial teams. A community team, amateur or professional, existed to provide hockey for the enjoyment of the community. A commercial team existed to make money. Community teams were owned by groups of well-wishers who were content to make or lose money as long as the team gave the community good hockey. Sometimes hundreds of people were involved. The Montreal Victorias, who represented the community tradition with distinction from 1872 to 1939, winning three Stanley Cups, were supported by the members of the Victoria Hockey Club. "During the 1930s, the club had about 500 members each paying $5 a year," recalls former secretary-treasurer Frank Carlin, now a scout for the Philadelphia Flyers. "Earlier there were many more." A few community clubs, the Kitchener-Waterloo Dutchmen for instance, were incorporated, although the shares were spread around and no one ever made any money. But most were constituted very informally. "Anybody could come to the annual meetings of the Port Arthur Bear Cats," says Edgar Laprade, "and I suppose if someone brought along enough friends he could get himself elected president. Not many people wanted the job. It was too much work." Community hockey was built on love of the game particularly, love of sport generally, and community loyalty. Commercial hockey capitalized on these sentiments for private profit. The difference was like that between a corner grocery store and a supermarket. Unfortunately, the community and commercial traditions were not compatible. In hockey, as in any other business, maximizing profits means increasing revenues and reducing costs, which means buying up the best players to attract large crowds, and eliminating competition to keep player salaries at a minimum and ticket prices at a maximum. Whereas the community tradition would have sustained hockey wherever it was possible, the commercial tradition would see to it that hockey survived only where it was profitable. So the advent of professional hockey was both good and bad for the game. On the one hand, it enabled players to become full-time athletes. On the other hand, it gave commercial hockey a decided edge.

The early hockey entrepreneurs had been rink owners who booked games between amateur teams like the Montreal AAAs and the Ottawa Capitals, keeping 50 per cent of the gate for themselves (before 1901 it was 67 per cent). In some cases, a rink owner would offer a slightly higher percentage to a team that undertook to play only in his arena. When professional hockey came along, some rink owners bought teams. J. P. Doran bought the Montreal Wanderers in 1909 and moved their home games from the Wood Avenue Arena to his own Jubilee Rink. But professional hockey created a new breed of hockey entrepreneur. He did not have to own a rink, because now it was possible to own the players. He hired the players and rented the arena, then took the difference between gate receipts and expenses as profit. George Kennedy, Sam Lichtenhein and Tommy Gorman, who founded the National Hockey League on November 22, 1917, in Montreal's Windsor Hotel, were such men. So was Eddie Livingstone, the man they excluded. Some were ex-hockey players, like Art Ross, Lester Patrick and Jack Adams. Some were playboys like Leo Dandurand. And some were millionaires like Ken Dawes, a brewer who owned the Montreal Maroons, grocery king Charles Adams, who owned the Boston Bruins, and banker John Hammond, who owned the New York Rangers. They all had one thing in common: a financial self-interest in building low-cost teams that would attract large crowds. They set out to make fortunes from hockey, and many of them succeeded.

Then, as now, commercial hockey was frequently characterized by salary wars. When P. J. Doran, Ambrose O'Brien, Jimmy Gardiner and Jack Laviolette founded the National Hockey Association in the fall of 1909 they desperately needed players, so they bought them away from other leagues, wooing Fred Whitcroft from Edmonton for $2,000, Lester and Frank Patrick from British Columbia for $3,000 each, and Cyclone Taylor from the Ottawa Senators of the rival Canadian Hockey Association for $5,250. (At the time, the highest paid player in all hockey, Tom Phillips of Ottawa, was receiving only $1,800 a year. The Senators soon decided they could not compete on these terms and within months joined the new NHA). Two years later, when Frank and Lester Patrick started the Pacific Coast League in Vancouver, Victoria and New Westminster, a salary war ensued that lasted almost 10 years. In 1911, 16 of the 23 players in the Patricks' league came from the NHA. In 1913, the Patricks offered contracts to every player on the NHA's Quebec City Bulldogs, the current Stanley Cup champions. Naturally, the NHA retaliated — the Montreal Wanderers signing goaltender Bert Lindsay and Walter Smaill of the Victoria Aristocrats in 1916, the Senators regaining Frank Nighbor from Vancouver. Once these wars were over, salaries would quickly return to normal. When the Canadian Hockey Association folded in 1910 the NHA limited total salaries to $5,000 per club, reducing average salaries from $1,500-$1,800 to $500 - $600. The new breed of hockey entrepreneur was quick to discover the cardinal principle of commercial sport: the teams in a league may be competitors on the ice but they are partners in business. So when there were commercial struggles, they were not so much between team and team but league and league. New leagues came and went with the winters. In 1909, the Eastern Canadian Hockey Association tried to drop the Montreal Wanderers and form the Canadian Hockey Association. That backfired when the Wanderers' owner, P. J. Doran, helped form the National Hockey Association and put the CHA out of business. But among the team owners in any one league efforts were made to strengthen weak clubs. When the NHL was formed in 1917, the teams were badly balanced. Competition was stiff from the amateur leagues for the loyalties of fans. So in 1920, the NHL broke up the leading Ottawa Senators and distributed the players among the other teams in the league, allowing them to return to Ottawa only for the Stanley Cup playoffs at the end of the season. The new hockey entrepreneurs raided not only other commercial leagues but community leagues as well. In 1906 the Ottawa Senators bought Smith Falls goaltender Percy Lesueur for their final playoff game against the Montreal Wanderers. The following fall,

Smith Falls decided not to ice a team and the Amateur Federal League, of which it was then champion, folded. Virtually every community in Canada can tell a similar story. In 1925 and 1926, the Port Arthur Bear Cats won the Allan Cup. Then Conn Smythe signed Bear Cat goaltender Lorne Chabot for the New York Rangers and Danny Cox for the Toronto Maple Leafs (which Smythe purchased after being fired by the Rangers). The Bear Cats did not regain the national championship until 1929. In the late 1930s, it took the Drumheller Miners several years to recover from the loss of the Bentley brothers, Max, Doug and Reg, to the professional leagues. The hockey entrepreneurs were allied with powerful capitalists like the O'Briens and the Daweses, and thus enjoyed a crucial advantage over community teams operating on a non-profit basis: a ready source of capital to buy players. In these circumstances, the community teams were on the defensive.

As commercial hockey prospered, it was only natural that the men who owned it would try to sell it in the United States. By the end of the First World War, the National Policy of Sir John A. Macdonald, which had encouraged trade along the east-west route of the CPR, was in difficulty. Macdonald, with his tariffs, had unwittingly induced a large number of American firms to locate branch plants in Canada, increasing north-south trade in manufactured goods. The flow of primary goods had begun to change direction, too. Canada was exporting ever-increasing amounts of iron and coal, newsprint, oil, natural gas and hydro-electric power — and most of it was going to the United States. In the absence of any countervailing action by the post-war Liberal government of Mackenzie King, the pattern of economic life in Canada was becoming increasingly north-south and it would have been remarkable if commercial hockey, which was, after all, just another business, had not followed suit. In 1916 and 1917, when the New Westminster and Victoria franchises in the Pacific Coast League folded, the Patrick brothers set up new franchises in nearby Portland, Seattle and Spokane. The Portland Rosebuds, Seattle Metropolitans and Spokane Canaries were the first commercial hockey teams in the United States. But it was in the eastern states that commercial hockey really took hold. While Europe struggled with post-war unemployment and inflation, the American economy boomed and the proceeds financed the Golden Age of American sports. (These were the heydays of Babe Ruth, Jack Dempsey, Red Grange.) American businessmen began bidding for hockey franchises, and the seven-year-old National Hockey League was only too happy to oblige. The first American franchise was sold to Boston's Charles Adams in 1924 for $15,000. He called his new team the Bruins. (An indication of the unimportance of NHL hockey at the time was the coverage the sale of the Boston franchise received in Toronto's *Globe*. The main story on the sport page the morning after it was announced was an account of Parkdale's 5-4 overtime victory over Kitchener in the senior Ontario Hockey Association. The Boston story merited only two paragraphs.) In 1925, Pittsburgh bought a franchise for $15,000. Its team was to be called the Yellow Jackets. And the same year the Hamilton franchise, players and all, was sold to Tex Rickard and New York's Madison Square Garden for $75,000. The Hamilton team, which Rickard renamed the New York Americans, had finished in first place that year. In 1926, the NHL sold three franchises: a second for $15,000 to New York, creating the Rangers; and one each at $50,000 apiece to Chicago and Detroit, creating the Black Hawks and the Cougars (later renamed the Falcons and then the Red Wings). In three years, the NHL had sold six franchises in the United States. In Canada it had sold one. In 1924, Ken Dawes, Thomas Arnold, Gordon Cushing and Jim Strachan paid $15,000 for a second Montreal franchise. The Maroons would play their home games in a new rink they had built called the Forum. Only the intervention of Conn Smythe prevented the sale two years later of the Toronto St. Patricks' franchise to a syndicate in Philadelphia. The American group offered $200,000. Smythe got the team for $160,000 by appealing to the nationalist sentiments of its owners, J. P. Bickell, N. L. Nathanson, Paul Ciceri and Charlie Querrie. "You fellows are good Canadians and you already have a terrific profit," he said. "Besides, you all live in Toronto and you have many friends. Surely you don't want to walk down the street in your home town and have the neighbours snub you because you sold out to foreigners. Haven't you any civic pride?" But for most of the new hockey entrepreneurs, men like Percy Thomson who sold the Hamilton franchise to New York, it was a great moment to capitalize. In 1926, Lester Patrick quickly dismantled the six-team Western Hockey League, selling all the players to new NHL clubs in the United States for $272,000. Not that Vancouver, Victoria, Edmonton, Saskatoon and Calgary could not support hockey (two years later Patrick re-established teams in Vancouver and Victoria). It was just that the opportunity for a quick, easy profit was too great. A buck is a buck.

The first casualty of the expansion of commercial hockey to the United States was the Stanley Cup. On March 18, 1892, the then governor-general of Canada, Lord Stanley of Preston, had anounced that "it would be a good thing if there were a challenge cup which could be held from year to year by the leading hockey club in Canada. I am willing to give a cup that shall be annually held by the winning club." The

Stanley Cup quickly became an event that every year brought together Canadians from different parts of the country, much as the Canadian football's Grey Cup does today. But in 1916, the Portland Rosebuds won the Pacific Coast League championship, and, as was the custom, challenged the National Hockey Association champions, the Montreal Canadiens, for the Stanley Cup. William A. Foran, the cup's trustee, saw no harm in it. Henceforth, he said piously, the Stanley Cup would be awarded to the "world champion". Losing the cup to the world would not have been so bad, but that is not what happened. Soon after the National Hockey Association became the National Hockey League, it began to look upon the Stanley Cup as its own. The cup had a value the NHL was not prepared to share. In 1928, the NHL was engaged in a player war with the American Hockey League, much like its battle today with the World Hockey Association. Tom Shaughnessy, who had been fired as manager of the Chicago Black Hawks, had nurtured the AHL to the point where in cities like Chicago, where he managed the Shamrocks, it was drawing crowds of between 10,000 and 15,000. In 1931, the AHL challenged the NHL for the Stanley Cup. NHL President Frank Calder protested. The NHL would rather forfeit the cup, he said, than play in such a series. The cup's trustees refused the challenge, and, unable to benefit from the prestige and gate receipts a Stanley Cup series would have provided, the AHL soon disbanded.

From the very beginning the NHL showed a predisposition to put economics ahead of hockey. Economics determined where the NHL chose to sell franchises. The Depression reduced the number of NHL teams to six. In 1930, the Pittsburgh Pirates became the Philadelphia Quakers and folded after one season. In 1934, the Ottawa Senators became the

St. Louis Eagles and they too folded after one season. The Montreal Maroons died in 1938, and the New York Americans, after four years of NHL trusteeship, were dropped in 1942. These were all economic decisions. The Ottawa Senators had been among the NHL's founding members, and sentiment might have dictated that instead of selling the team to St. Louis the league should have attempted to put it back on its feet. Economics dictated otherwise. The same was true of new franchises. There was a time in the early 1950s when the NHL considered granting a franchise to Québec City, where the Québec Aces with Jean Beliveau were drawing 15,000 fans a game. It had nothing to do with the desirability of another Canadian franchise. It was simply a question of whether a team in Québec could make money. Economics dictated rule changes as well. In 1928, to increase hockey's popularity with unsophisticated American audiences, the league accelerated the pace of the game by instituting penalties for "ragging" the puck and by permitting forward passes in all three zones. Up until that time, forward passing had been permitted only in the zone between the two bluelines, so that to get within shooting distance of the goal a player had to stickhandle past opposing defencemen. The redline, which further accelerated play, was not introduced until 1943 to compensate for inferior war-time players. By 1949, Frank Boucher, its originator, was calling for its removal. Economics necessitated an ever-lengthening NHL schedule. In 1917, it was 22 games. It was extended to 24 games in 1921-22, to 30 games in 1924-25, to 36 games in 1925-26, to 44 in 1926-27, to 48 games in 1931-32, to 50 games in 1942-43, to 60 games in 1946-47, to 70 games in 1949-50, to 74 games in 1967-68, and today it is 78, not including exhibition and playoff games. Each extension was justified on the grounds of rising salary costs. Even the Stanley

Cup playoffs were contrived out of economic need. After Lester Patrick sold the Western Canada League in 1926, there was no one to challenge the NHL for the Stanley Cup. So a system was devised (in 1927, six teams qualified) that would sustain interest and revenues well beyond the end of the regular season. Some of these playoff series stretched out so long and the refereeing in some of them was considered so erratic that on at least two occasions — in *Maclean's* in 1936, and in *The Canadian Magazine* in 1939—Henry Roxborough, one of the most respected sports commentators of his day, was compelled to defend the NHL against charges that professional hockey was fixed.

The most tragic consequence of the NHL's economic imperative was its success in monopolizing hockey. Essentially, it was a question of eliminating competition. The NHL granted each of its owners the right to veto any application for a second franchise in his city or its environs, an effective guarantee against commercial competition. In 1931, the Chicago Black Hawks stopped the sale of the Ottawa Senators to Chicago hockey promoter Tom Shaughnessy on just such grounds. But community hockey was still a threat, and here the NHL employed what is known in business today as "product differentiation", which means establishing in the minds of consumers a distinction between your product and your competitor's. Product differentiation is usually achieved through advertising, but the NHL did it by manipulating the press. Newspapers were persuaded to devote more space to NHL hockey at the expense of the amateur leagues. Frank Selke, the Kitchener electrician who went on to become one of the most successful managers in NHL history, tells a story in his autobiography, *Behind the Cheering,* about the Toronto Maple Leafs' first pre-season training camp. "The physical rewards of early season training were great," wrote Selke, "but of greater importance was the fact that our team practically eliminated Senior and Junior amateur hockey gossip from the sports pages. Everybody suddenly became Leaf conscious." The name of the game was publicity. Leave readers with the impression that NHL was better. Product differentiation.

But product differentiation works only if it has some basis in fact, and the owners of the NHL were smart enough to realize that they could not rely on impressions alone; ultimately they could draw away fans from community hockey only by giving them something better, and they could only do that if they owned the best players. Those they did not already own, they could try to buy, but that would be expensive and — worse — uncertain. Far better simply to establish a proprietorial claim to hockey players everywhere, so that those you want are automatically yours. That is what they did. In 1927, after a series of conferences between NHL President Frank Calder and senior amateur clubs, five new professional leagues were established — the Canadian Professional League (Windsor, Niagara Falls, Hamilton, London, Stratford, Kitchener, Detroit, Toronto); the Canadian-American League (Providence, New Haven, Boston, Springfield, Québec, Philadelphia); the American Hockey Association (Minneapolis, St. Paul, Duluth, Winnipeg, Kansas City); the Prairie League (Edmonton, Calgary, Saskatoon, Moose Jaw, Regina); and the California League with four teams in Los Angeles — all having working agreements with the NHL which gave it rights to any players it wanted. It might have ended there, with the NHL controlling professional hockey throughout North America, except for the Depression.

The economic collapse of the Thirties was disastrous for commercial hockey. None of the five leagues established in

1927 survived. But community hockey thrived. This was its Golden Age, and for obvious reasons. NHL salaries were low, player opportunities uncertain (remember, three NHL teams folded in seven years), and a player who signed a professional contract could never return to amateur play. Community hockey did not pay as well, although a few players like the Montreal Royals' John Acheson were able to make the equivalent of an NHL salary (in 1938, Canadiens' owner Ernest Savard complained that some amateurs in Montreal were making *more* money than the NHL players). But there were compensations. Community hockey was steady, it meant less travelling, it guaranteed an off-season job, and it did not require you to leave your home town. Diversions were few in those lean years so the stands were always full, even at 50 cents a ticket. In Montreal, the Wednesday night and Sunday afternoon doubleheaders with the Royals and the Vics always drew a full house in the Forum, while the more expensive Canadiens drew barely 5,000. Few teams cancelled their schedules because of debt. So by the end of the decade, the community leagues once again dominated Canadian hockey and once again threatened the owners of the NHL. "It is an open secret that the practical operators of the NHL are not completely sold on [the CAHA's decision to allow 'amateurs' to be paid]," wrote Ralph Allen in *Maclean's* in 1940. "The CAHA is now, in effect, running a vast professional league, a league that is strongly entrenched, not only in the big cities, but in a score of relatively new fields like the colliery country of Cape Breton, the manufacturing empire at Oshawa, the rich mining belt around Sudbury and Kirkland Lake and farther west at Geraldton and Flin Flon, Saskatchewan wheat towns like Yorkton and Weyburn, bustling coal and oil strongholds in Alberta like Lethbridge, Drumheller, Olds and Turner Valley, and in British Columbia, fruit or smelter centres like Nelson, Kimberley and Trail. The reaction around the NHL was of studied horror. It was unfair competition, that's what it was. More than one NHL governor hinted darkly that unless the whole sinful project were abandoned, the NHL might call off its various agreements and start a war."

The struggle between the NHL and the CAHA never materialized. The Second World War intervened. After France fell to the Nazis in 1940, hundreds of players, amateur and professional, enlisted. Within the next two years, the NHL would lose 90 players to the armed forces. War regulations made it difficult for Canadians to continue to play hockey in the United States. For instance, the Rangers' Brian Hextall, having been granted an exemption from military service on the grounds that he was a farmer, was ordered by the Saskatchewan War Mobilization Committee to stay in Canada and farm. Still the NHL survived, pressing into service teenagers like Ted Kennedy, Don Raleigh and Ted Lindsay and retired players like 42-year-old Frank Boucher, who played 15 games in 1943-44 after retiring in 1938. The Canadian and American governments helped considerably, permitting the NHL to use players in the reserve, and relaxing travel restrictions on NHL teams. For the community teams it was different. Many of them ceased operation. Allan Cup competitions continued for a while, but it was service clubs with professional players that won them (an RCAF team led by Boston's Kraut line of Bob Bauer, Milt Schmidt and Woody Dumart in 1943, the Ottawa Commandos with Turk Broda in 1944). In 1945, the Allan Cup playoffs were cancelled. By the end of the war, senior community hockey had lost its momentum. Some of Canada's hockey players did not survive the war, and not all of those who did wanted to play again. Industry was booming, jobs were plentiful, and after years of fighting in Europe, many of them de-cided to settle down and raise families. Nor did they always return to the communities they had left. The war accelerated the exodus from towns to cities, defence production having spurred industrial growth in the country's large urban centres. Those who did want to resume playing hockey were des-perately needed by the NHL and the numerous professional teams that had sprung up in the United States and the United Kingdom after V-E Day. War-time changes in the game ac-centuated the player shortage. While the redline sped up the game, it also highlighted the growing disparity in playing ability, so most teams added another forward line and a pair of defencemen to compensate. "If we had to play against the Kraut line all the time," Conn Smythe once confided to Ted Reeve, "the score would be 10-0." After years of inactivity, the community teams could not compete, and many of them never operated again. By 1951, the calibre of senior hockey had deteriorated to such an extent that the national cham-pionship was divided into two categories: the Allan Cup for smaller towns and poorer clubs, and a new trophy, the Alexander Cup, for the few major cities that still had senior teams. Three years later, the Alexander Cup championship was discontinued. Conventional wisdom has it that senior hockey died in Canada with the advent of television in the 1950s, but by the time television arrived the community tradition was already dead. It died with the Second World War, and senior hockey died with it.

In that article in *Maclean's* in 1940, Ralph Allen had warned that "if hostilities [between the NHL and the CAHA] are ever instituted, the best either organization can hope for is the worst of it". As it turned out, war with the CAHA was now unnecessary. Having the upper hand, the NHL could simply buy the CAHA off. In 1940 the NHL made an agreement with the CAHA, offering $250 for every player it signed from the community leagues and another $250 if the player made it on to an NHL roster. In 1945 the agreement was amended to make the signing fee $500 for players taken by the NHL and $250 for players taken by the minor professional leagues. As soon as the war ended, the NHL began developing its sponsorship system. With the consent of the CAHA, every NHL club and every minor professional affiliate was permitted to sponsor two junior teams, owning the rights, of course, to their players. The result was the "chain" system sanctioned by the CAHA in 1947, which gave junior clubs an interest in encouraging players to sign with the NHL. The converse was also true: young hockey players were now discouraged from pursuing any course other than making the NHL, especially continuing their education and playing university or community hockey. The country's best junior players were grabbed up by the NHL before the senior teams could even approach them. To make sure no player got away, the NHL denied the community teams the reserve clause which the NHL enjoyed: "No contract or agreement other than simple registration as a player, made between a player and any member club of the CAHA," read the agreement, "shall be binding upon or have any effect whatsoever upon the [NHL] or its duly affiliated or associated minor leagues." The 1947 agreement made the CAHA the instrument of the NHL. As a special committee of the National Advisory Council on Fitness and Amateur Sport observed in 1967: "If any organization is to operate independently, it must enjoy control over its own procedures. For a sports governing body, this means it must be able to determine the eligibility of its own members, the playing rules of its competitors, and it must be free to determine how to spend its own funds. The Canadian Amateur Hockey Association enjoys fully none of these essential rights." The NHL had turned Canadian amateur hockey into one big farm system.

Nineteen-forty-seven was the NHL's thirtieth anniversary, and it had cause to celebrate. For all intents and purposes it now owned hockey in Canada. It had eliminated its major source of competition, the senior community leagues, and it now managed most of the junior clubs that produced the country's young players. All that remained was to enjoy the profits. And this it soon began to do. And has been doing ever since.

In 1910, George Kennedy bought the Montreal Canadiens for $7,500. Eleven years later, his widow sold the club to Leo Dandurand, Joseph Cattarinich and Louis Letourneau for $11,000. In 1935, the Canadian Arena Company, which owned the Montreal Forum, purchased the team for $165,000. Controlling interest was held by Senator Donat Raymond. No purchase price was disclosed when the Molson family bought Senator Raymond's interest in 1957 but *The Financial Post* estimated the Canadian Arena Company's worth at $2.7 million. Forty-eight hours before the federal government imposed a capital gains tax on January 1, 1972, the Molsons sold their 58 per cent of the company's shares for an estimated $15 million. That represents a 14-year profit of $13.5 million, plus annual dividends amounting to about $3 million. Owning a piece of the Toronto Maple Leafs has been just as profitable. Maple Leaf Gardens Ltd. issued its first shares in 1931 and began paying dividends in 1934. It has not missed a year since. In 1936, Gardens stock was selling for $1 a share. If you had bought 100 shares then, they would be worth $18,750 today. In 1961, John Bassett joined the late Stafford Smythe and Harold Ballard in buying Conn Smythe's controlling interest in the Gardens. Bassett's share of the purchase price was $900,000. Ten years later he sold his stock to Smythe and Ballard for $6 million. It is almost like printing money. In August, 1972, the Gardens declared a $3 dividend, and Harold Ballard, now the largest single stockholder, collected $1,540,000. In one year, $1,540,000. Think of the money the Smythes, Molsons, Bassetts and Ballards have taken out of hockey over the years.

Throughout its history the NHL has been a model of economic initiative and enterprise. As a business it has been successful beyond anything its founders might reasonably have expected. But the issue is not whether a business should do whatever it feels necessary to prosper (although even that is arguable). The issue is whether hockey, which is a part of our culture, should be operated as if it were just a business, like the manufacture of razor blades. The answer is no.

Everybody Makes a Buck

Dave Keon yesterday attracted more than 100 advertising and industry executives to an informal reception at the Royal York Hotel, where they met Dave Keon and Associates. The associates, of course, were not men like Leaf linemates Garry Monahan and Bill MacMillan, or any other players, but such key people as Ron Hewat, the broadcaster, Keon's voice and image coach, and business partners Billy Harris, Harry Neal and Mike Elik . . . . Keon stood around saying hello. Later, while associates spoke of him in glowing terms, he ran over the notes of the speech he and Hewat had prepared. Hewat spoke first. He told everybody the purpose of the gathering wasn't to go over Keon's statistics. Everybody knows about his hockey. "This is to introduce you to Dave Keon the man. What we call the total package. The name Dave Keon generates excitement." And this excitement can sell products, Hewat continued, as it is doing for Jelinek skates and other companies. "Dave Keon, the businessman, has arrived in Toronto," Hewat concluded.

—Dan Proudfoot, The Globe and Mail, *March 17, 1971*

The owners sell tickets and television rights, a little booze, a lot of peanuts, popcorn and Cracker Jack, and unnecessarily lavish programmes. The players sell their services as athletes, for which they are paid about $45,000 a year. That is an average figure. Some make less, some more. But the money that changes hands inside the arenas is only the beginning. Hockey today is a marketing tool. Its popularity is exploited to sell everything from cars to shaving lotion, a process that has contributed in no small way to its present low estate.

The owners have always been in hockey for the money. Only recently have the players become greedy, turning the game into a commercial brothel by offering themselves as salesmen to anyone with something to sell. Bobby Orr pitches Yardley colognes. Bobby Hull pitches Mercuries. Henri Richard pitches Skil power tools. Dave Keon pitches Campbell soups. Derek Sanderson pitches Riviera slacks. Red Kelly pitches loans from the Associates. Phil Esposito pitches Kraft macaroni. It is the rare hockey player who does not have a piece of the action, even if it is only his picture in some car dealer's advertisement with the caption: Special Sales Representative. Guy Lafleur was being hustled by advertisers almost from the day he was drafted by the Montreal Canadiens. His business manager, Gerry Patterson, said, "We declined the endorsements. We'll review them in a year for a programme beginning in two years. Now we are considering life insurance, tax situations, estate planning."

Bob Haggert runs a company called Sports Representatives Limited, which procures commercial endorsements for about 50 NHL players including Bobby Orr, Frank Mahovlich, Yvan Cournoyer, Ron Ellis, Ed Giacomin, Mike Walton, Marcel Dionne and Dale Tallon. He started the business in 1968, quitting a job as head trainer with the Toronto Maple Leafs. "The basic thing," he told a reporter one day, "is that the popular professional athlete remains the easiest vehicle with which to enter homes. He's welcome, whether he's telling you about a product on television, in print, or if he's on a personal appearance at a car dealership or supermarket." It works like this. You run a company that manufactures corn flakes. Your advertising agency decides to build a television campaign around a hockey player. The psychology is simple: "If Bobby likes them, they must be good." So the agency calls Haggert or someone like him and together they choose the man for the job. Maybe they decide to use a number of players — a French Canadian in Québec, a Toronto Maple Leaf in Ontario, a Vancouver Canuck in the West. The players are chosen, make the ads, and that is that. You do not have to find players who actually like your corn flakes, because organizations like Sports Representatives can supply players who are willing to endorse a product whether they believe in it or not. If you sold laxatives instead of corn flakes, they probably would not touch you (it wouldn't be good for the image), but the only taboos are tobacco and alcohol — prohibited by the standard NHL player's contract. It does not matter whether your corn flakes are better than your competitor's or even worth eating at all. There are players who will sell them for you anyway — if the money is right.

It is a rip-off. The fans admire hockey players for their skill as athletes. They pay them well for it — the fans, after all, buy the tickets and pay the television costs passed on by sponsors. The players accept their admiration and then turn it to selling red convertibles. It is like going to church and having the minister try to sell you a refrigerator. Perhaps the players are unaware that they are doing anything wrong. They get into hockey young. They are treated like chattels from the time it is apparent they have talent. From the beginning they are taught to think of hockey as a means to an end, just another and better way of making a buck. So when someone comes along and says he will pay them a few thousand dollars just to stand in front of a television camera for half a day, it does not even occur to them to ask why. What is the difference — playing hockey or making television commercials, it is all money. But by joining business in the exploitation of hockey — instead of fighting it — they become businessmen themselves. With press agents, office managers and tax accountants.

In the United States, endorsement income is taxed at a considerably lower rate than conventional earnings. Stamps, envelopes and the autographed pictures players send to fans are tax-deductible. Hockey players are beginning to learn these things. While he was still playing hockey, Gordie Howe became a partner in a cattle ranch in Michigan. Polled Herefords, he told a reporter one day, are a good tax shelter. Bobby Orr, who owns (among other things) part of a hockey camp, a car wash, apartment projects, various common stocks, a farm and a condominium in Florida, says hockey players "have come to realize the potential of making their money grow. I'm no great businessman, but I'm learning." Orr's hockey school, which is owned by a holding company called Bobby Orr Enterprises, is a $300,000, 180-acre camp on the shores of Lake Couchiching in Ontario. During the summer about 1,000 kids, most of them from the United States, spend a week or two learning hockey at the camp — which at something like $130 a week makes it a nice little investment. There are hundreds of such schools in Canada and the United States. Howe has one. Jim Pappin has one. Allan Stanley has one. The Esposito brothers have one. Yvan Cournoyer has one. Roger Crozier has one. Jim Gregory and Wren Blair have one. Billy Harris and Dave

Keon have eight, maybe more by now. In the last five years hockey schools have become a $4.5 million-a-year business.

No one begrudges hockey players financial independence. For years they were the poorest paid athletes in professional sport. Those were the days when Stanley Cup winners were given rings instead of bonuses. But $45,000 a year is more than a living wage, enough certainly that hockey players should not have to extort a dollar from everything they touch. A few years ago, Phil Esposito's lawyer said *Maclean's* would have to pay $1,000 to use Esposito's byline on an article the magazine wanted to ghost-write for him. "How can I ask manufacturers to pay thousands of dollars to use Phil's name," he said, "and then turn around and give it to *Maclean's* for nothing?" Not long after, Esposito and Orr refused to appear at a New Hampshire benefit because the organizers would not pay them $1,500 apiece. (Baseball player Joe Torre, the National League's top hitter and most valuable player, attended for $500.) The typical professional hockey player today puts a dollar value on everything. The wonder is that he does not charge for autographs.

The tragedy is that the player-businessman is an anti-sportsman. He mocks the efforts of duffer and serious competitive athlete alike. Thousands of Canadians are rediscovering physical culture — swimming, running, playing football, golfing, hiking, curling and skiing. But they are a minority. Most Canadians are still afraid of sport, regarding it as unpleasant medicine good for losing weight, disciplining children and rehabilitating cardiac patients. They agree with A. J. Liebling that *mens sana in corpore sano* is a contradiction in terms. The hockey player, the most influential athlete in the country, could encourage more people to discover how good it feels to participate in sport. Instead, he reinforces the belief that sport has no intrinsic worth. He does not play the game for fun, he plays it for money. And if only a handful of young Canadians are willing to dedicate their lives to becoming Olympic champions, it is because there are not enough adult athletes in Canada setting an example. The hockey player sets exactly the opposite example: with a few exceptions he is a complacent performer who prefers the racetrack to the training room. He does not have the time or the inclination to be the best in the world — he is too busy making money. The New York Rangers' Vic Hadfield said it all during the recent series between Team Canada and the Soviet Union: "With off-season activities to look after, I don't think we would be able to work at it 11 months a year the way the Russians do."

But the players are only recent partners in the commercial exploitation of hockey. Business has used our love of the game — just as it uses sex — to sell its products for years. The Imperial Oil Company has been a sponsor of NHL broadcasts for so long, first on radio and then on television, that it is impossible to see an Esso sign and not think of hockey — which is exactly what Imperial Oil intended. Shortly after the Molson family bought the Montreal Canadiens in 1957, *The Financial Post* speculated that what it was really after was a shot at sponsoring the Canadiens' telecasts. What hockey had done for Imperial Oil it could also do for Molson's beer — and has. But at least Imperial Oil and Molson's offer the telecast in return. What about the company that hires Bobby Hull to skate around like an idiot with shaving cream all over his face? Or the company that has Bobby Orr taking slap shots with a pen through his stick? What do they contribute? And what about the manufacturers who use NHL insignias to attract sales? In 1966 the NHL created a subsidiary called National Hockey League Services. It sells licences to manufacturers permitting them to identify their products with the NHL or one of its teams. A few years ago there were only seven or eight licences. Today there are about 50. They include manufacturers of watches, jewelry, golf balls, mechanical hockey games, jigsaw puzzles, ceramic mugs, glassware, giftware and various articles of clothing. It is great for the manufacturers and the NHL, but it degrades the sport.

If there were an award for the most vulgar exploitation of hockey, it would certainly have gone to the Power Player promotion concocted for Imperial Oil in 1971 by a company called National Sales Incentives. Power Player stamps were like the hockey cards kids used to buy in packages of bubble-gum. One Power Player stamp came with every $3 purchase at an Esso station. The pitch was simple: get the kids to get their parents to fill their tanks with Esso. Toy manufacturers employ similar techniques in the television ads they run for children on Saturday mornings. "Hey kids, ask mom and dad to get you. . ." Using children to nag their parents to pull in at the Esso sign is bad enough, but Power Players were a cheat besides. There were 252 players in the NHL, but you could buy a million dollars worth of Esso Extra and all you would get was 192 of them. Sixty were never issued. If a kid wanted a complete collection, his dad had to spend 75 cents and buy a Saver Stamp Album, in which there were photographs of the 60 missing players. If he wanted the real thing — that is, not just photographs but actual Power Player stamps of the 60 missing players — his dad had to buy the Supersaver book for $4.95. Power Players were a great commercial success. They brought Imperial Oil new business, and as for National Sales Incentives, its founder, a man named Harvey Kalef, was said in 1971 to be worth $16 million.

Money, as they say, does not grow on trees. When someone is making a fortune, someone else is losing one. In this case, the someone else is the Canadian hockey fan. He is the consumer to whom all these money-making ventures are aimed. They sell, he buys. Everyone makes a buck. Everyone but the fan. He pays.

Hockey has always been special for Canadians, one of the cultural forms we all know and care for. But now it is used for something for which it was never intended: it has become just another come-on. No cultural form, be it education, painting, music or hockey, can be so systematically debased and still retain its self-respect. We are still as passionate about hockey as we ever were, but we have learned to rationalize its growing inferiority. "Hockey's just a business now," we tell ourselves to explain away the disappointment of a boring game. It is an apology we should never have to make.

The Cheerleaders

It is unfortunately a fact that the quality of performance on Canada's sport pages is too seldom on a par with that in Canada's sport arenas. The profession is still burdened with hacks who make tin-can gods out of cast-iron jerks. I believe there is still a tendency among sports reporters to slant news in favour of the home team, to defer to local sports management for the sake of maintaining cordial working relationships, and to accept publicity handouts in place of digging for their own stories.

— *Dick Beddoes, sports columnist for* The Globe and Mail, *testifying in Ottawa before the special Senate committee on the mass media, March 3, 1970.*

Owning an NHL hockey team means never having to spend a buck on promotion. The press flogs the game for nothing.

It was Sunday, April 6, 1969, and the Boston Bruins had just defeated the Toronto Maple Leafs four games straight in the 1968-69 Stanley Cup quarter finals. Punch Imlach, coach and general manager of the Toronto club for eleven seasons, stood dejectedly in the corridor between the dressing rooms at Maple Leaf Gardens. Boston stars Bobby Orr and Derek Sanderson walked by as they came off the ice. "Good luck, Bob," said Imlach, but Orr did not hear him. Sanderson stopped and was shaking Imlach's hand when Stafford Smythe, the late president of Maple Leaf Gardens and the Toronto Maple Leaf hockey club, turned the corner. Imlach spotted him and disappeared into his little office. Smythe followed. "Would you mind leaving us alone for a few minutes?", Smythe asked reporters and closed the door. The substance of what the two men discussed in private was contained in a front-page headline in *The Globe and Mail* the next morning: "Smythe fires Imlach, Tulsa man new Leaf coach."

Perhaps Imlach vowed that very night to get even with Smythe for dumping him in so public and humiliating a way. But it was not until he was appointed coach and general manager of Buffalo's new NHL franchise more than a year later that he revealed his mission to the world. Shortly before the June, 1970, draft, at which the Buffalo Sabres came into being, Imlach told reporters, "When they draw up that schedule, circle the date when Buffalo plays its first game in Toronto. That'll be the night." The schedule was drawn up in September. The date was November 18.

Everything pointed to a bad game. The Leafs were still floundering after a last place finish the previous season. They lost their season opener to the fledgling Vancouver Canucks. On their first extended road trip, they were beaten by Los Angeles, Oakland and Vancouver. As for Buffalo, except for goalie Roger Crozier, rookie Gil Perreault and veterans Phil Goyette and Don Marshall, the Sabres were a team of has-beens and also-rans and what, in the aftermath of NHL expansion, are charitably called "journeymen" hockey players. It should have been one of those games at which, as you walk into Maple Leaf Gardens, you hear not "Who's got a pair?" but "Who *wants* a pair?"

But Imlach knows how to use the press. He plays hockey

reporters the way Glenn Gould plays the piano, and this was a virtuoso performance. He was turning a mere hockey game — and a game between two last place teams, at that — into a public duel. "If ever a guy wanted to win a hockey game," he told reporters, "I want to win this one. I'd give anything to jam this one right down his [Smythe's] throat." It was going to be Punch Imlach against Stafford Smythe, the working stiff against the rich guy, the faithful employee against the boss' son, the guy with the funny name Imlach against the WASP named Smythe. Imlach knew he could sell it to the press. He had been around professional hockey a long time, long enough to know that the newspapers would be looking for stories to run in advance of Buffalo's first game against the Leafs. In feeding them lines like ". . . Smythe told me that one of the reasons I was let go was that I was too old, and I told him 'I'll stuff that down your throat,' and believe me, that is my objective" he was just making it easy for them.

They went for it. This is from Red Burnett, writing in the *Toronto Star* on November 17:

When Punch Imlach received his National Hockey League schedule, he ringed November 18, the night his Buffalo Sabres pay their first visit to Maple Leaf Gardens. He'd love to hand his old club a pasting. Discussing tomorrow's game, King Clancy, Imlach's sparring mate when Punch was the big hockey boss in these parts, said: "Brother, would I love to be able to sit in on Punch's pre-game spiel to those Sabres. He'll take the paint off the wall in the visitors' dressing room." Imlach, however, insists there'll be no verbal thunder from him prior to the game. "I'll just say, you know how I feel about this game, how much it means to me for you to play well."

The late Charley Barton's story in the Buffalo *Courier Express* on November 18 went like this:

TORONTO, Ont. — The tickets read "NATIONAL HOCKEY LEAGUE, Toronto vs. Buffalo, Wednesday, Nov. 18, 1970." For George (Punch) Imlach, it's the World Series . . . the Super Bowl . . . the Kentucky Derby . . . all rolled into one. For C. Stafford Smythe, it's a Holy War . . . a vendetta, personal and meaningful . . . a chance to sink another harpoon where it can do the most damage . . . and where it will hurt the most. Whatever it is, tonight's first meeting of the Sabres and the Toronto Maple Leafs is far from just another game in the National Hockey League's 546-game schedule. This will be the first of six games between the Sabres and the Maple Leafs and the first time Imlach will send a club against the Leafs since Smythe, the embattled and abrasive Toronto president, fired him a year and a half ago. Imlach guided the Maple Leafs to four Stanley Cups in 11 seasons, yet Smythe, fretting anxiously in the wings, waited only seconds after Boston knocked off Toronto in the playoffs two years ago before unfrocking him . . .

And in his hockey column in the *Toronto Telegram* of November 18, Imlach got to tell the story himself:

Tonight must be listed as one of the most memorable occasions in my career. I must say I am a little apprehensive wondering how the fans will react. The Toronto fans have been accused of sitting on their hands. . . . The timing is fantastic, both tied for last place. Naturally, it could be better — they both could be tied for first place. Buffalo Sabres naturally are the underdogs, an expansion team playing an original club, playing away from home with plenty of injuries

. . . . I notice that Stafford Smythe is now going on the road and will lend support to the coach. Stafford gave me as one of the reasons for firing me that I was too old to coach his team. . . . About that too old bit, I told him at the time I would stick it down his throat. Tonight is my first chance.

Imlach could not have stage-managed the game more perfectly if he himself had hand-lettered the signs "Punch is Number One" and "Punch is Best" that hung the night of the game at either end of Maple Leaf Gardens. It was standing room only, and even John McLellan, Imlach's successor as the Leafs' coach, described the demand for tickets as "fantastic". When Imlach stepped out of the Buffalo dressing room a few minutes before the teams took the ice, he was mobbed by well-wishers. A peanut vendor came over and shook his hand. "Do me a favour," he said, "and beat those Leafs." The Gardens fans gave him a standing ovation when he made his entrance, and they were still cheering him two and a half hours later when, the Sabres having humiliated the Leafs 7–2, he returned to the Buffalo dressing room. "Did I shove it down far enough?", he asked reporters. "Did I?" It had not been much of a hockey game, but the crowd left the Gardens that night laughing and obviously pleased. In the press box at McMahon Stadium, 2,000 miles away in Calgary, where reporters were covering a playoff game between the Calgary Stampeders and the Saskatchewan Roughriders, the news of Buffalo's victory was greeted by a big hurrah.

An "advance" is a story about an event *before* the event. It is not peculiar to hockey or even to professional sport. The entertainment pages of any newspaper are full of them. When Columbia Pictures or American International is ready to release a new film, it will send one of the stars on a "promotional tour". She will go from city to city, always a few days ahead of the movie's opening, talking to the press. Not that she has anything to say, but it works. In the paper the next day, there will be a big picture of the star and beneath it a story that will invariably contain the line, ". . . who was in town yesterday to publicize her new movie, which opens at the . . . ". The point about an "advance," as any movie producer or NHL manager will tell you, is that it is better than an advertisement because not only is it cheaper, it is more believable.

No one knew that better than Conn Smythe, Stafford's father and the founder of the Toronto Maple Leafs. The elder Smythe is still venerated as the man who built Maple Leaf Gardens in the midst of the Depression by paying the workers 80 per cent of their wages in cash and the remainder in Gardens stock. (It is less well known that, because stock would not put bread on the table, he was able to buy a lot of it back at 25 cents on the dollar.) He did not invent the hockey "advance," but very early on he persuaded the Toronto hockey writers to cover the Leafs' practice the day before a game, assuring them a story the day of the game. One day one of the papers missed a practice, and Smythe was peeved. So he summoned the other two and gave them a story, something about a trade, perhaps, or a new Leaf prospect. The paper that did not get the story got the message. Smythe still chuckles about it. "I taught them a lesson. You have to cover the practices. You have to be there if you want to find out what's happening." The three Toronto newspapers have been attending Leaf workouts regularly ever since. "They haven't found a new way to practice," says Toronto *Sun* columnist Ted Reeve, "but we cover every practice just the same."

The most common hockey "advance" is the interview with

one of the players, but it is only one variation on a theme performed monotonously wherever hockey is played professionally. Don't miss tonight's game, goes the refrain, because it is your first chance to see the NHL's new wonderboy Guy Lafleur. Or, Boston has not won a game in Toronto since 1969, and tonight may be the night the Bruins break the jinx. Or, there was a real Donnybrook the last time Vancouver played Toronto and both teams are preparing for a rematch. Or, with the Canadiens and the Rangers tied for fourth place, tonight's game is a four-pointer. Or, tonight's game might give some indication as to the outcome of a Stanley Cup series between these two clubs. And on and on. Always the message is the same: tonight's game, folks, is compulsory.

Perhaps it is stretching it to say that "the quality of performance on Canada's sports pages is seldom on a par with that in Canada's sport arenas". Not all our sports writers are "hacks who make tin-can gods out of cast-iron jerks". Still, hockey promoters like Imlach could not get away with selling bad hockey at $7.70 a seat if they did not have the press to help them. And it is no exaggeration to say that poor reporting has been an accomplice to hockey's demise.

The traditions of North American sports writing are all wrong. The sports pages and sportscasts are parades of interminable statistics, scores which have consequence only for bettors, and gee-whiz interviews that perpetuate the image of the athlete as over-grown kid. "Home runs by Mike Epstein and Joe Rudi led an 11-hit barrage off three pitchers as Oakland Athletics defeated Baltimore Orioles 5-2 last night." . . . "After holding B.C. to one yard in the first two plays of the game, Calgary struck fast with a touchdown at 3:26. The big play was a 51-yard pass from Keeling to Kerr." . . . "The dream of golf's Grand Slam is gone for this season, so Jack

Nicklaus is flirting with a new goal — $300,000 in winnings in a single session." . . . "Feagan has 126 wins on the Ontario Jockey Club circuit this year, and appears to be headed for another 200-plus season." . . . "Phil Roberto took a bad beating from Bobby Orr in the third period. Orr bounced off the boards and caught Roberto with a solid right as Phil turned away. The rest of the fight was no contest." It all sounds the same. Not that stats, scores and personalities are not a part of a sport, but that is all they are: a part. Sport is also technique, strategy and, no less than any other aspect of our lives, ethics. These the sports reporters by and large ignore.

Technique is what separates good hockey players from the rest of us and good hockey games from the kind we see too frequently in the post-expansion NHL. A good move or a good play, even if it does not result in a goal, even if it amounts to only one second in 60 minutes of hockey, is often the most exhilarating part of any game. And yet accounts of these moments rarely figure in the press' coverage of hockey. A few years ago the Boston Bruins were playing a Sunday afternoon game in Toronto, and at one point when the Bruins were shorthanded Bobby Orr invented a new play. He was standing with the puck behind the Boston goal. A Leaf forward skated in after him, so he started up the ice toward his own blueline, the Leaf forward in pursuit. It is a routine play. But instead of continuing up the ice or passing the puck to a teammate, he turned suddenly and took the puck back behind the goal to safety. When the Leaf forward came after him again, he did the same thing again, starting up the ice and then wheeling quickly back behind the goal. He did it four times before it dawned on the Leafs to send two men after him, one from each side of the goal. In those few seconds, Orr had added something to hockey. It was not a bad game, but it was otherwise unexceptional, and a story could have been written about the game describing nothing but that one innovation. Had it ever occurred to Orr to try it before? Had he been practising it, or did he make it up on the spot? How often does a hockey player create something new? The papers the next day did not even mention it. Orr has a move at the blueline on Boston power plays, a pirouette towards the boards, an evasive action to elude opposing forwards that leaves him wide open for a shot on goal. Millions of words have been written about Bobby Orr, about how much he makes and what kind of car he drives, about his home, his family and his friends, but no one has ever written a story about that move. No one has ever written a story about *how* Bobby Orr plays hockey. "Bobby Orr is fast" . . . "Bobby Orr can do everything" . . . "Bobby Orr is the greatest" — that is what passes for technical analysis of the most talented practitioner of hockey among the people whose business it is to write and talk about it.

Not that intelligent analysis is not possible. A few years ago Hugh Hood wrote a book about Jean Beliveau called *Strength Down Centre,* in which he described the Montreal centre's technique on faceoffs:

We took eight or ten faceoffs together, with Gerry Patterson [Beliveau's business advisor] dropping the puck. Jean's stick-action at the faceoff is difficult to describe. When I watched it happen, the comparison that immediately occurred to me was the motion of a small snake's tongue. Those little snakes are often seen around summer cottages, and they catch insects on the ends of their tongues, with the tongue sliding in and out so fast that you can barely see it. That's the way Jean moves his stick: he must have wrists of incredible

143

*strength and sensitivity, because he doesn't just get the puck,
he can put it precisely where he wants it. . . . The movement
of his wrists and the blade of the stick is simply too fast to
see. We took one after another and Jean would call his shot,
"Left wing. To the point. In front of the net. Shot on net."
And he put the puck exactly where he called it every time.
Not within a foot of where he intended; exactly where he
intended, just like a billiards champion. The delicacy of the
wrist and arm motion must be quite a lot like that used in
handling a cue, infinitely accurate.*

No, it is not that it cannot be done, or that the members of
the hockey press are not knowledgeable enough to do it. They
are. It is just not part of the tradition.

It is the same with strategy. Hockey is a more spontaneous sport than football, baseball and basketball, so knowing strategy is not as important to an appreciation of the
game as it is in those other sports. Still, as anyone knows
who has watched two opposing hockey coaches juggle lines,
there is more to winning hockey games than giving the players
a pat on the back. Emile Francis has reasons for sending
out Walter Tkaczuk and not Jean Ratelle against Phil Esposito — but what are they? The sports pages never tell you.
According to Gordie Howe, every team in the NHL plays
Boston heavy to the right side when Orr is on the ice, trying
to clutter his lane and force him to pass the puck. There are
hundreds of such strategic ploys, as critical to the outcome
of any hockey game as the relative talents of the players,
but all you get from the sports pages are scoring plays, injury
reports, fight summaries, and the leavings of dressing room
gossip. In 1967, the Toronto Maple Leafs defeated the
Chicago Black Hawks in the Stanley Cup semifinals, and a

factor in the series was the way the Leafs' Brian Conacher contained Bobby Hull. This the hockey writers acknowledged — "Conacher did a great job checking Bobby Hull" — but they did not explain how he did it. Here is how Conacher himself explained it in his book *Hockey in Canada*:

I knew that if I played Hull too cautiously he would walk all over me. I also knew that if I tried to match him in a foot race I would lose miserably. Hull had a tendency to skate well back into his end of the rink, sometimes even behind his own net, to shake off his opposing winger and give himself some skating room. I knew that if he did this with me, and I waited to pick him up at the blueline again as he came out of his end, I was dead. . . . So I decided that the only thing I could do was stay with him wherever he went, even if it meant following him to the washroom. . . . A lot of players tried to stop Hull with brute force. In most cases they lost . . . Hull is tremendously strong and I knew that I would lose . . . if I tried. While he was cruising in his end of the ice trying to get a play going, I was going to skate with him continually . . . but I knew I had no hope of ever catching up with him if he got away from me. To defend against this happening, I did not stick right at his elbow, but played him fairly loosely. I planned to stay close enough to him, say four or five feet away, so I would be there every time one of his teammates passed the puck to him, but not so close that he would get that extra stride on me if he decided to break away. The last bit of defensive strategy I used was to try and keep myself between Hull and our goal. I knew that if I ever got behind him, there was no way I would ever catch him short of him breaking his leg.

Conacher could have told all that to reporters, and they could have passed it on to their readers. Instead, they wrote advances for the Leafs' next series against Montreal.

Never was the superficiality of hockey reporting in this country more apparent than in the reports that preceded the recent eight-game series between Team Canada and the Soviet Union. Virtually every hockey writer in Canada incorrectly predicted an easy Canadian win, when a careful analysis suggested quite the opposite. Many of these same sports writers had witnessed first hand the results of the Russians' determined and scientific approach to sport in the Olympics. Many of them had covered international hockey where it has been obvious for years that European teams, not just Soviet teams, would soon be strong enough to challenge the NHL. The Russians never made any secret of the way they planned to beat the NHL. Anatoli Tarasov, the coach emeritus of the Russian team, had described it in a book published in Canada in 1969. He had talked about it in countless newspaper interviews. A full week before the series opened in Montreal, Lloyd Percival, who had talked with Tarasov, discussed the strategy the Russians were confident would give them an edge against the Canadians. Still, the Canadian press gloated over what was to be a certain Canadian victory. It was the NHL party line they had been rewriting for years.

But if sports coverage in Canada is deficient in its neglect of technique and strategy, it is doubly so in its neglect of ethics. Dick Beddoes, *The Globe and Mail* sports columnist, sometimes refers to the world of professional sport as "the playpen". That is his way of saying that its inhabitants — players, coaches, managers, owners *and* reporters — behave as if the rest of the world does not exist, as if a football game is as important as an election. There is the playpen and there is the real world, and for the people in the playpen what happens in one has no bearing on the other. The playpen operates by its own rules and moral conventions. Athletes are not supposed to have political views and neither are the reporters who write about them. That is why the sports press is generally uncritical. In how many breathless reports of Bobby Hull's $2.8 million contract with the Winnipeg Jets did the writer or broadcaster speculate as to how much ticket prices would have to be raised, how many more television commercials would have to be squeezed in, to pay the inflated salaries hockey players like Hull are now demanding? A couple of years ago, Hal Sigurdson, a hockey writer with the Vancouver *Sun*, wrote a story about the Canucks' Rosaire Paiement. The headline read: "A little Fergie in punchy Paiement."

The first thing Rosaire Paiement wants understood is that his home town is Earlton, Ont., not Haileybury, like it says in the National Hockey League Guide. "Oh, I was born in Haileybury, all right," Rosie admits, "but that's only because Earlton is so small we don't have our own hospital." Thus, not only is Earlton Rosie's home, but also the home of his four brothers and 11 sisters, which may explain why the rugged right winger is quickly establishing himself as the light heavyweight champion of the NHL. A guy learns to be fast on his feet when he has to share a bathroom with 11 sisters.

The pugnacious Canuck has developed his own effective on-ice brawling technique, partially through experience, and partially through careful study of the style of Montreal's John Ferguson. "Most guys I fight are taller than me," he explains, "so they have the longer reach. Now when I fight, I try to grab the guy by the sweater with my left and pull him in close to hit him with my right. . . . That's the way Fergie does it."

Though he's only five-foot-10 and 178 pounds, the former Philadelphia Flyer doesn't back away from any of the league's heavyweights. During the course of his first season in a Vancouver uniform, he has taken on Vic Hadfield of the Rangers, Gerry Korab of Chicago, Ron Harris of Detroit and Bob Kelly of Philadelphia. Thursday in Boston, Paiement twice tangled with the Bruins' wonder boy, Bobby Orr. And though the Canucks were 8–3 losers, Rosie had to come out ahead. In the first skirmish only two punches were landed, both over the shoulder of a linesman. Orr connected first, then Paiement shot out a right that cut Bobby for seven stitches over the left eye. In the second battle, Orr eventually wrestled Paiement to the ice, but not before Rosie's quick hands had re-opened the same cut.

But as far as Paiement is concerned, hockey fights are not to be taken personally. "Orr? I think he's just great. Sometimes I'd just like to be able to sit in the stands and watch him play." So why does he fight? "To tell you the truth, I just love it," he grins sheepishly. "What the heck. You know what you're doing, you don't get hurt. Look at me, not a mark on me." But despite his frequent battles, Earlton's most prominent son insists he doesn't start many of them, which, as he admits, is a trifle out of character. "Well, I did start one. In the first Toronto game. I started the fight with (Garry) Monahan, but that's just because I figured we needed something to get us going."

One of the few NHL heavyweights Paiement hasn't tested is the man whose style he's copied. "But I'd like to go with Fergie," he says. "I'd like to see just how good he really is. It's . . . you know . . . a challenge."

Fighting is not a part of hockey — at least it is not supposed to be. Sigurdson would condemn anyone who admitted he enjoyed beating up people in the street. But he apparently condones the pleasure Paiement takes in giving Bobby Orr a seven-stitch cut over the eye. The only way Paiement can beat Orr is by bullying him, but if the NHL does not disapprove, why should Sigurdson?

In the absence of criticism, sports reporting becomes little more than free advertising. Most hockey writers and broadcasters are simply press agents for the owners of professional hockey. Virtually everything they write or say is calculated to enhance the game's popularity. Dr. Bruce A. McFarlane, Professor of Anthropology and Sociology at Carleton University, came to that conclusion some years ago when he was writing his MA thesis on the relationship between sports writers and sports promoters in Montreal:

It is generally assumed that sports reporters, like other reporters in their respective fields, go out and gather newsworthy material for their newspapers. It is further assumed that they will be continually on the lookout for scoops, digging up news and objectively reporting it to the readers. However, because of the nature of the social organization [of the professional sports world] . . . this is impossible. Indeed, the ability to dig out news is almost a liability. Because of the obligations, personal and financial, owed by the sports writers to the promoters, they find themselves in the position of "rewrite men". That is, they are "permitted" only to write up stories that have been issued as releases or items of news sanctioned by the promoters.

It would be wrong to blame the reporters for all this when in fact their employers, the people who own the media, are

149

more at fault. In the early days of professional hockey, newspaper men were poorly paid and easily bribed. Self-righteousness did not feed a family or buy a drink. Many a sports writer was grateful for the little brown envelope a club owner slipped him on Fridays. All he had to do to earn it was write what he was told. Everyone knew about it, including the publishers, but if it meant they did not have to raise reporters' salaries, what was the harm? Times have changed. Journalists formed unions and today are well paid. They can afford respectability. A television set may occasionally change hands, but nobody picks up an envelope on Fridays. That does not mean the press is no longer bought and sold. John Halligan, who is employed as a publicist by the New York Rangers, covers the occasional out-of-town game for the *Post,* New York's only afternoon newspaper. The Canadiens and other clubs in the NHL pick up travel expenses for hockey writers on the road (some newspapers insist on paying their way, but not many). Some reporters line up with the players for out-of-town meal money. In the interests of "good publicity," the NHL has for years given some hockey writers free rides to the Stanley Cup playoffs. So it is the owners of the media, not their reporters, who take the payoffs today. If a dollar saved is a dollar earned, the publisher or station owner whose employees travel at the expense of a hockey club is pocketing more money than any reporter ever collected in a little brown envelope.

Years of payoffs have produced a climate in which the hockey press sees its interests and those of professional hockey as identical. McFarlane's thesis quotes a Montreal sports editor: "It's like a marriage. It's like a big happy family. That way it's beneficial to everybody. They'd be out of business without good publicity. We'd be out of a job." Most hockey reporters operate under the assumption that what is good for professional hockey is good for every-one. The few who believe differently are subjected to intimi-dation.

Stan Fischler, whose syndicated hockey column appears in Canadian newspapers, began his career as a sports reporter with the late New York *Journal American*. He had always loved hockey, so it was a dream come true when in 1964 he was given the hockey beat. The Rangers had trouble starting that fall. They lost their first home game, and at the bottom of his story Fischler mentioned that some of the New York fans had begun to chant "Muzz must go." (Muzz Patrick was then the Rangers' general manager.) The game was on a Wednesday night. Fischler's story ran on Thursday. On Friday, he called the Rangers' publicity office, just mak-ing a check, and was informed that henceforth he would not be admitted to either the New York dressing room or press room. When he asked why, he was told that the Rangers did not like his coverage of their opening game. The *Journal American* was an afternoon newspaper and, according to the tradition, the story for an afternoon paper is always in the dressing room or press room. The reporter for a morning paper can write about the game, but the reporter for an afternoon paper is expected to come up with a post-game angle. He can usually find one talking to the players in the dressing room or to the coach or general manager in the press room. What the Rangers were trying to do, then, was cut Fischler off. They were making it impossible for him to function as the *Journal American*'s hockey man. He recalls thinking to himself, "Jesus, here I've been waiting to get this beat all my life and now, after covering only one game, they're kicking me out. What's my editor going to think?" The sports editor of the *Journal American* was a man named Max Kase. Fischler told him what had happened. Kase could easily have knuckled under and put a new man on the beat. That is what the Rangers wanted. But Kase knew that in the marriage of convenience between the newspaper and the promoter, the promoter's need is greater. The Rangers needed the *Journal American* more than the *Journal American* needed the Rangers — New York, after all, is a baseball town. So he phoned the Rangers and told them that until Fischler's dressing room and press room privileges were restored they would not get a line in his newspaper. On Sunday night, Fischler covered New York's second home game of the season and after the game was admitted to the dressing room and press room.

For nearly 10 years, starting in the middle 1950s, Fischler was New York correspondent for *Hockey News*, a tabloid published weekly during the hockey season by Ken McKenzie, who also owns a magazine called *Hockey Pictorial,* and who was at one time the NHL's publicity director. It was never a very happy association. "McKenzie was constantly warning me — and I mean constantly — not to get anybody mad, because in hockey it's not done. In hockey you have to write nice things." But Fischler did not listen — to McKenzie or to anybody else. Muzz Patrick, coach Phil Watson and publicity man Herb Goren called him into the Rangers' office one day for a friendly chat. The message was the same: a little less ginger. Finally, in 1964, Fischler started hearing reports that William Jennings, the Rangers' new president, was unhappy with his articles in *Hockey News*. "So I decided to confront him, and I called him up, and the gist of his remarks was that nobody else who writes for *Hockey News* ever criticizes the home club and we're not going to tolerate it from you." *Hockey News* appointed a new New York correspondent shortly thereafter. "I asked Mc-

Kenzie why, and he told me that my writing was too critical, and he did not want to chance losing the goodwill of the owners."

Losing the goodwill of the players can be just as problematic. Ted Green has never forgiven Fischler for publicly criticizing his excessively pugilistic style of play during the 1964-65 season. Fischler telephoned him about something one day not long afterward. "You've got a fucking lot of guts, calling me," Green said and hung up. And maybe he passed the word, because afterward Fischler discerned a growing coolness on the part of the entire Boston organization. A profile on Orr for *Sport* magazine brought Fischler to Boston the following December. The Bruins were playing the Canadiens, and he wanted to see the game so he called Herb Ralby, who was both the Bruins' publicity man and the hockey writer for the *Boston Globe,* to get tickets. Ralby said the best he could do was tickets for Boston's next home game against Oakland. "It was obvious to me that he was trying to shaft me. So I called Don Ruck, vice-president of the NHL, and he managed to get me a ticket through Charlie Mulcahy, the Bruins' vice-president." But it did not end there. After the game, Fischler went down to the Bruins' dressing room to talk to Orr and was stopped by Ralby. "He said, 'You're not allowed in the Bruins' dressing room,' and later I pursued the matter and he was right. It lasted two years."

Fischler's experience is not unique. Dick Beddoes, who plays the gadfly with relish (he once wrote of Punch Imlach that he "reached puberty but forgot to touch second base") has been similarly ostracized. "Will I be welcome in the Gardens coffee shop the next day? That's the feeling," says Beddoes, "that prevails among the guys on the beat who — let's give them this — have to work with these people, the players and coaches and general managers. They have to maintain a pipeline. Those who won't be manipulated don't get the handouts. When you won't be manipulated, you miss the off-the-record briefings. And you get sleazy whispering campaigns. 'Beddoes is a sonofabitch,' they'll say. 'You can't trust him with information.' Or, 'Beddoes is cheating on his wife.' 'Beddoes is a reformed lush.' It may start with a coach or a general manager, maybe even in the press box itself. The fact is, if you do this profession as honestly as you can, you wind up with very few friends in the Establishment." Beddoes has paid for his sins. In 1964, the CTV television network was launching a weekly sports show called *Sports Hot Seat,* and the network's sports consultant, Johnny Esaw, told Beddoes he was going to be one of the panelists. "He wanted me on the show because that's my style," says Beddoes. "I take people on." At some time he must have taken on John Bassett, publisher of the Toronto *Telegram,* owner of CFTO-TV, a director of the CTV television network, president of the Toronto Argonaut football club, and at the time the largest individual stockholder in Maple Leaf Gardens, which owns the Toronto Maple Leaf hockey club. *Sports Hot Seat* went on the air without Beddoes, and much later Esaw confided to him, "I'm sorry, but there was no way Bassett would allow you on this show." "It shows how they handle you," says Beddoes. "If I had in some way subdued what I was saying in print and been a nice fellow, I'd probably have got the work. The guys that did it got pretty good money."

No one knows better than Scott Young the consequences of breaking step with the NHL. Young was writing a sports column in *The Globe and Mail* in October, 1962, when the story broke that Chicago Black Hawks' owner Jim Norris had offered the Toronto Maple Leafs $1 million for left winger Frank Mahovlich. It was a publicity stunt, and Young said so. He wrote:

The word for the so-called Mahovlich deal was H-O-K-U-M. Hokum, bunkum, nonsense, guile, delusion, gullery, bluff, hanky-panky, sham, make-believe, spoof, hoax, bamboozle, gerrymandering and humbug. The definitive statement was delivered by Stafford Smythe a few minutes after the gag was born last Friday night in a hotel room which was not being used for a general meeting of the Woman's Christian Temperance Union. "We'll get the World Series out of the sport pages tomorrow morning," Smythe called out, laughing.

Had he stopped there, Young would not have got into trouble. But later in the same column he went further:

But some people can't let a good joke die. They have not noticed that vaudeville is dead. That is the only interpretation that anyone should place on the fact that John Bassett, another Leaf director, lent his manly quotes to a front-page story in his newspaper [The Telegram] yesterday. He said that when the Leaf directors considered the offer formally (presumably if they could keep straight faces long enough), he would recommend that the offer be accepted. This statement was being read in his newspaper at precisely the time that he was conferring with Smythe and [Harold] Ballard and deciding, with them, that the offer would be rejected. The official communique on this meeting was couched in the language which generals use to explain strategic retreats with honour to all and malice toward none. There wasn't so much as a "hee, hee" to place the matter in its proper perspective.

That was too much for John Bassett. He had Young taken off *Hockey Night in Canada*. "These are very tough guys," says Young. "They will fight you with any means at their disposal, without it ever becoming a personal thing. They will tell you to your face that you're full of BS. If you have a valid point with which they disagree, they will do everything within their power, including keeping you off television and out of certain publications, anything that is within their power to do they'll do to keep you from expressing it publicly. They simply feel they're defending their business against an attack that might hurt it. Now, in actual fact, the attack has yet to be devised that can hurt professional hockey. The most telling criticisms have been made against the sport, all well documented, but nobody gives a Goddamn. The people keep on beating down the doors to get in."

Fischler and Beddoes and Young have continued to write about hockey, despite harassment. Intimidation works only if the reporter knuckles under, so in the end the responsibility to report the bad with the good falls on him. "After all," says Young, "all the Establishment can do is lay themselves open to your laughter. If Clarence Campbell is cool to me when he happens to run into me in the press room or somewhere, I report it and it's laughable. And nobody is ever denied information, not really. The general managers are so competitive that if you can't find something out from one you can find it out from another. The players, for all the nominal control the owners have as to how they must physically spend their days, are under no such discipline when it comes to what they think. I could go into any hockey club and find out what I wanted to find out whether the coach wanted to tell me or not, because there are always three or four guys who will talk to you even if they don't know who you are. But there are other writers who are self-censors, which is the worst form of censorship. Guys who are always thinking in advance, 'Is this going to offend anybody?' "

Self-censorship. On a September morning in 1970 a veteran Toronto hockey writer was sitting in the blues at Maple Leaf Gardens watching coach John McLellan put the Leafs through a morning workout. A younger man sat down beside him. They talked for a while about the Leafs' prospects, about the players who would have to come up with good seasons if the Leafs were going to make the playoffs. "What do you think of McLellan?" the younger man asked. "Is he a good coach?" "Yeah, he's a good coach," the veteran replied, "but he's got too many people second-guessing him. Most coaches in the league only have to worry about the general manager and maybe the owner. McLellan has Jim Gregory, the Leafs' general manager, Stafford Smythe, who owns the club, and King Clancy, too. So what's he going to do? He's just come up from the minors, for the first time in his life he's making a good dollar, he's probably bought a house with a $40,000 mortgage in the suburbs. What's he going to do? Tell them to get off his back? How can he?" It was a more illuminating explanation of McLellan's dilemma than the veteran hockey writer ever gave his readers.

The consequences of a compromised press are more serious than the public's ignorance of the burdens of a professional coach. In allowing themselves to be used as cheerleaders, mouthpieces to be manipulated by men whose primary interest is making money, the reporters who cover hockey have assisted in transforming it from a Canadian sport into a branch of American show business. Had they spoken up, had they really believed in that cliché about the press being the eyes and ears of the people, the NHL might not have been able to take unchallenged control of Canadian hockey. It might not have been able to strangle community hockey in Canada. It might not have been able to kill the National Team. If they had cared more about hockey and less about the patronage of men who buy and sell it, they might have spared us the humiliation of witnessing our national game being sold to the Americans.

But there is more at stake than our national game. The sports pages are probably the best read pages of any Canadian newspaper. For most of the year they are dominated by hockey. Garry Smith, a sports sociologist at the University of Western Ontario, found in a recent analysis of a single week's sports coverage in the *Edmonton Journal* that 699 of 1,527 column inches, or 46 per cent of the sports news in the *Journal* that week, were devoted to hockey. The hockey writer is the most influential spokesman for sport in the country. More than anyone else, he teaches us the meaning of sport. If he is uncritical of capricious violence, if he registers no disapproval of the slashing, interference and boarding for which professional hockey players are no longer penalized, if he fails to challenge such flagrant abuses as the 78-game regular schedule, if he applauds the win-at-all-cost ethic enshrined in professional hockey, he contaminates our attitudes towards all sport. Vince Lombardi, the late and much-lionized coach of the Green Bay Packers, is famous for the epithet: Winning isn't everything; it's the only thing. But there is another concept of sport, far more exhilarating and infinitely more enlightened. No one has described it better than René Maheu, director general of UNESCO: "Sport is an order of chivalry, a code of ethics and aesthetics, recruiting its members from all classes and all peoples. Sport is a truce: in an era of antagonisms and conflicts, it is the respite of the gods in which fair competition ends in respect and friendship. Sport is education, the truest kind of education — that of character. Sport is culture because it creates beauty and, above all, for those who usually have the least opportunity to feast upon it." For more than half a century, the press has condemned Canadian sport to the perverted world of Vince Lombardi.

Bringing the Game
Back to Life

Since we have a Canadian pro football league that seems to function rather well in competition with the NFL/AFL, why not have a Canadian pro hockey league? Resurrect the Ottawa Senators, the Montreal Maroons and Toronto St. Pats (the latter two cities could easily support two pro teams). Add such cities as Quebec, Hamilton, Halifax, Winnipeg, Regina, Calgary, Edmonton, and Victoria. I'd bet my bottom dollar it would succeed.

— George G. O'Leary of Ottawa, in a letter to Maclean's, *December 1970.*

If we cannot save hockey, we cannot save Canada. Think about it for a moment: As problems they are remarkably similar. Canada is becoming a colony of the United States. We supply the Americans with raw materials and energy, they supply us with the finished product, making us dependent on them not only as a market for our exports but as the source of our consumer goods. The people who run the country rationalize this dependency by telling us we do not have the resources to develop the country ourselves — a lie — and that therefore it makes more sense to sell it for what Prime Minister Trudeau calls "good hard cash". The same is true of hockey. A game nurtured by generations of Canadians has been sold to Americans. And again we are told that, in terms of profits, it could be no other way. "To stay in business," Clarence Campbell likes to say, "you place your operations in places that will keep you in business." So what happens? Many of our foremost artists and scientists have been forced to leave the country because government and business have not provided work for them here, and many of our best athletes, our hockey players, have been forced to become migrant workers in the United States. It is such an everyday occurrence we take it for granted. "A professional hockey player," says *Weekend* magazine's Andy O'Brien, "is a man with a skill to sell, like a doctor or an engineer, and we'd hardly regard a doctor as disloyal for heading to a hospital in Miami or an engineer for accepting dam-building contracts in South America. If 11 American cities offer whopping salaries to Canadians to do the thing they do best, why shouldn't they go? If they're really good we'll see them on TV." So hockey, and Canada, are caught in the same dilemma. The NHL sells hockey in the United States because Americans have more money to pay for it. Canadian businessmen sell their firms to American corporations (even when it means fewer jobs for Canadian workers) because American corporations pay higher prices. In the end, then, survival is question of who chooses. Do we allow businessmen to make these choices for us, or do we make them ourselves? If we sit by and do nothing, hockey is lost — and Canada, too. If, on the other hand, we decide that some things belong to all of us, not just to the men who ostensibly own them, then maybe it is not too late. Maybe there are enough of us who believe that we would be better off if we controlled our own country ourselves. If so, we should do something about it. And maybe reclaiming our national sport is a good place to begin.

We cannot save hockey unless we are prepared to do two things. First, we must sever the chains that bind the Canadian Amateur Hockey Association to the National Hockey League, so that we can begin once again to teach Canadian boys to play hockey, not NHL hockey. And second, we must start a professional hockey league of our own.

A Canadian professional hockey league would bring the sport back to life in cities that once enjoyed it and now go without: Victoria, Calgary, Regina, Saskatoon, Thunder Bay, Sudbury, Windsor, London, Kitchener-Waterloo, Hamilton, Sherbrooke, Saint John and Sydney. Imagine a 24-team, three-division (east, central and west) league, with teams from those cities and from Vancouver (two teams), Edmonton, Winnipeg, Toronto (two teams), Ottawa and Montreal (two teams). The season is 44 games (plus playoffs), each team meeting every other team in its division four times and every team in the other divisions once. The teams are owned by the communities themselves. The players are paid salaries between $25,00 and $30,000 a year.

The success of such a league is dependent on two assumptions. The first is community ownership. Clarence Campbell is right: the majority of Canadian cities cannot support hockey — as long as it is played to make money for the men who own the teams. No one would be willing to buy an NHL franchise in a place like Thunder Bay when he can get a larger return on his investment in a place like Philadelphia. But does hockey have to be run as a business? Should it be? It belongs to all of us, not just the governors of the NHL. We pay for the rinks, the equipment, the ice time and the coaching. If our kids become hockey players

165

rather than pole-vaulters or bull-fighters it is because we tell them it is important. Hockey meant something to us long before the NHL and Imperial Oil invented *Hockey Night in Canada.* The money the NHL gives the CAHA for player development would not pay the annual minor hockey ice bill in Toronto or Montreal, so why should the NHL be allowed to harness this community investment for private profit — profit reaped mainly in another country? Professional hockey in Canada should be operated as a public utility. If it were, the surpluses of teams in larger and richer centres like Toronto could be used to subsidize teams in smaller, less affluent communities like Thunder Bay. The point is, professional hockey *can* be supported in communities smaller than Vancouver, Toronto and Montreal if the league is community owned.

The single biggest cost in operating a professional hockey team is salaries, which bring us to our second assumption: that it is not necessary to pay hockey players $100,000 a year. Community-owned teams could afford to pay salaries between $25,000 and $30,000 a year, which would put the players in the top 5 per cent of Canadian wage earners. Community-owned teams could not compete with the six-figure salaries players are being paid in these heady days of competition between the NHL and the World Hockey Association, but maybe they would not have to. Maybe we misjudge the professional hockey player in thinking that his only concern is the buck. After all, what choice does he have? If he wants to play professional hockey, he has to play for the NHL or the WHA and what else have they to offer? In the kind of league we are proposing, he could play hockey in Canada, perhaps in the community where he grew up, and playing only 44 games a season, instead of 78, he could really play the game, play the best hockey he is capable of playing instead of merely putting on a show. If we are wrong in this, if hockey players care more for money than for the sport and their home towns, then a Canadian professional league would not stand a chance. But if that is the case, what hope is there for hockey? And, by extension, what hope is there for Canada?

A community-owned professional hockey league would re-establish hockey as a sportsmanlike game, played in the pursuit of excellence rather than money. It would produce better hockey players than the NHL or the WHA, better conditioned, better coached and better motivated. It could provide us with a national team capable of regaining our former prominence in international hockey competition. A team of all-stars, assembled every four years for an entire season, could represent Canada in world championships. It would be no less professional than the team the NHL threw together for the recent series against the Soviet Union, but it would represent Canada better.

The idea of a community-owned professional hockey league in Canada is admittedly novel, but once launched there is no good reason to believe it would not work. We have the fans to support it — despite the low estate of NHL hockey today, Canadians still watch it for want of anything better. And we have the players to build it — every year minor hockey in Canada produces new players of undisputed talent whose only option now is to play for the NHL or the WHA. How would such a league fare in competing with the NHL and the WHA for the affections of Canadian fans? The Americans produce better football players than we do. The National Football League plays better football than the Canadian Football League. And yet Canadian fans still support Canadian football.

But a professional hockey league of our own is not

enough. Hockey will never be ours as long as the NHL, or any other privately owned professional league, controls amateur hockey in Canada. Kids will never learn to play the game for fun, to pursue hockey to any level they want — amateur, professional or whatever — until we stop running minor hockey as if it were a farm system for the NHL and the WHA. The CAHA must be liberated from its financial dependence on the NHL. Only the government, by providing the funds the CAHA needs to operate, can do it. We must also build more rinks and arenas, so that hockey is no longer a game for only the very young and the very talented. We must establish a national hockey institute, perhaps attached to one of our universities, so that we can develop skills, strategy and training methods suitable to Canadian conditions and experience. (In the aftermath of the recent Canada-Russia series, too many hockey people have suggested that we simply mimic European methods.) Such an institute would develop the means to eliminate unnecessary violence from the game. Perhaps fighting should result in an automatic game misconduct; perhaps a penalized player should be required to serve his full time, whether a goal is scored against his team or not; perhaps a penalized team should be prohibited from icing the puck. And finally, such an institute would develop and conduct a national coaching programme, so that the best methods of teaching hockey could be passed on in a systematic way throughout the country.

All of these recommendations have been made before — by parents, coaches, newspapers, civil servants and service clubs. But the CAHA and the government have been afraid to act, afraid of the NHL. In June, 1971, Health Minister John Munro received a confidential report commissioned from John Meagher, a professor of physical education at the University of New Brunswick, which called for the appointment of a commissioner to police amateur hockey in Canada. Rather than act on it, Munro commissioned another study six months later. We cannot depend on the CAHA, the government or Hockey Canada. Nor should we fear the NHL. The emperor has no clothes, as the recent Canada-Russia series made embarrassingly clear. Hockey belongs to us — parents, players, coaches, fans — and if anything is going to be done, we are going to have to do it. It should not be difficult. While the NHL controls professional hockey, we control — at least, we *can* control — the amateur leagues which produce the players. In 1972, every single player graduating from the Ontario Hockey Association Junior "A" was drafted by the NHL. If we can develop that many players for Clarence Campbell's league, we can develop them for a league of our own. Nor should we despair of our coaching strengths. The NHL may be bankrupt, but Canadian hockey is not. There are hundreds of coaches in this country who care about hockey, who are capable of innovation, but who have dropped out of hockey or, like Lloyd Percival, have been dropped. Maybe we cannot change things at the Montreal Forum, Maple Leaf Gardens and the Pacific Coliseum, but we can clean up the game at the neighbourhood rink. It is our game. If we want it back we will have to take it back.